Vacation Rental

Passive Income Through Smart Vacation Rentals Investing

(The Business Guide to Personal Autonomy and Financial Success)

Janice Anthony

Published By **Tyson Maxwell**

Janice Anthony

Vacation Rental: Passive Income Through Smart Vacation Rentals Investing (The Business Guide to Personal Autonomy and Financial Success)

ISBN   978-1-77485-722-9

Legal & Disclaimer

TABLE OF CONTENTS

Introduction

It's an exciting moment! Airbnb and other similar apps have allowed people like me and you to be hoteliers, or "hosts." Many may make use of their property assets to begin this business or buy a house specifically to be used for this reason. The opportunity available today makes it possible for anyone to be a J. W. Marriott.

Before we begin I'd like to clarify something as with everything else: there isn't anything about hosting a vacation rental so easy or attractive as it appears. Hosting can be filled with pitfalls to traverse, and you'll need to return to one piece after several blow-ups. This is the reason this book is all about: dealing with the easy transactions as well as those that aren't so smooth. Through anecdotes, I'm hoping to show the reader how to consider, react to situations and be proactive in arranging to be successful and how to keep your success going in spite of all the drama that could and will occur during your time in the field of vacation rental. The stories are real--only the names have changed. They're intended to illustrate a mindset that is reflected in a conduct code me and my staff follow for our properties to be packed, our guests delighted and our sanity in check.

I'd like to let you know the people this book was intended for, before we go over how the book is organized. This doesn't mean that everyone can take advantage of these strategies and apply them but let me sketch an outline of the reader who should read this book. There are ways to overcome this and solutions, so don't be discouraged in the event that you don't fit into the various categories listed below.

Remember that every step is founded on professionalism and good business practices. Remember that guests are customers and hosting is an enterprise! Do not be misled by hospitality terminology. As a host you're in charge of making your customers or guests as satisfied as you can. The customer always has the upper hand. Hosting is the fusion of hospitality, architecture interior design and sound business practices. There is no need to know everything in any of these areas, just eager to learn and bring in experts when you need to.

The intention of this book is to be informative and tactical and easy to understand guidelines that you can follow exactly or tailored to your requirements. After a certain amount of time it becomes automatic. There is no have to think about what interactions I have to make every day, week, quarter or year in order for my business. The goal of this guide is to guide you into a similarly efficient and financially profitable business. It doesn't matter if you're a full-time holiday-home owner with a home exclusively for renting, or an occasional host who lets out a room in a condo every once in some time There are some helpful suggestions and tricks to be found here which will make your reading enjoyable. We hope everyone has the best success in becoming the Master of Vacation Rentals!

Chapter 1: Fantastic Finds

The word "location" is synonymous with Location--this is the mantra you hear in the world of real estate to the point of being a cliché. There's a reason why this phrase is used every so often. It's crucial to think about when choosing the location of a house you'll to lease out. If you don't currently own a property you're looking to put on Airbnb There are numerous things to consider when selecting your next location.

"Most people don't look when they spot the needle in the grass. I'd keep looking to see if there are more needles"

--Albert Einstein

Vacationers looking for a vacation rental are making their way to explore your area. What draws people to your region? Consider using an app such as Yelp to find the most sought-after nightlife spots, such as places for dining or areas of clubs and bars big movie theaters malls, shopping centers, tourist destinations like historical or museums--the list could go on and on. If you situate your property somewhere central to a number of these spots, guests are more likely to look up the location and say, "That's perfect!" Proximity to public attractions and amenities, ideally within walking distance, is also a worthwhile consideration--though the prevalence of services like Lyft and Uber has made it easier to lodge at destinations farther away from areas of interest.

Don't think about the convenience of your guests for a moment. What about yours? Consider the proximity of a home to your main residence. If you're planning on making changes, cleaning, conducting maintenance, welcoming guests, giving keys away or keys. It's unlikely that you'll need to commit to an hour-long drive to complete every little errand, regardless of whatever the property is. Be aware that as a homeowner you'll be accountable to keep the house full of things such as dish soap, toilet paper fresh towels, and other essentials. If you're forced to make lengthy journeys to run errands can begin to drain your energy quite quickly.

Would you be able to make the trip out to your house in one day? How about getting to the destination and returning within one day? If your property in the satellite area requires an extended drive, be sure you have an welcoming guest who will stay for the night near your rental property. The cost of hotel rooms is a great way to make a dent in your profit potential. Property managers are able to manage local guest's needs in the event that and when they aren't present.

Remember that there are things to consider concerning neighbors homeowner's associations, neighbors property taxes local laws, many more.

* Can short-term stays be allowed? If yes, how are they controlled?

* What's the maximum amount of guests that could be accommodated at any given time? What do the maximums are based on? Certain are based on the bedrooms' number like.

* Are there any noise restrictions that guests have to adhere to?

Limits on the number of cars can be parked in the driveway? In the street?

Consider your neighbors! How far is the next house to yours? If you're in a structure which is thick, how thick are the walls? Are there any other units that are on all sides? What amenities could have to be shared (trash chutes laundry rooms, elevators or mail rooms) and where are they? Based on these design questions What are the chances for your guests likely to interact with or disturb your neighbors, and in turn, vice versa? Are there privacy barriers , such as hedges or fences? What do neighbors think about the increased traffic in your property?

A third and crucial aspect is to be aware of making forecasts of any upkeep or maintenance costs you may be faced with. Do you has a swimming pool? If yes, then be sure to consider the expenses for cleaning the pool as well as heating, chemicals and other types of maintenance.

There are a myriad of options that could result in unexpected utility or maintenance costs Some of them include:

* Carpets

* Hardwood floors

* Decks

* Heating/air conditioning

* Garbage disposals

* Landscaping/gardens

* Lighting, barbecues, and other outdoor amenities

* Septic tanks

* Entertainment systems

* Additional food storage like a second fridge or deep freeze

* Garage doors

Find out the average cost of utilities in your area before making the option of buying. For instance when you live in a warmer area air conditioning could dramatically increase the cost of electricity.

Other areas of financial and practical danger to be navigating could include:

* Tax impacts

* HOA fees

* Local ordinances and rules

* Airbnb's service charge

* Insurance

* General maintenance

It's time to think about something deeper than the daily aspects The WOW factor. It's an aspect that's difficult to define however it can transform an area of the ordinary and functional to something extraordinary and memorable. Amazing views, vibrant and innovative decor, gorgeously designed grounds--all of these types of features can cause the words "Wow!" from excited guests. This is a great sign. It signifies that your property be rated highly in the reviews of the ambience and aesthetics, but it's likely to also be featured on a variety of social media site, giving you free publicity!

If you want to increase that wow-factor, the most effective approach would be to allow nature take care of the work. If you live in an area with a deck overlooking a beautiful Lake in the mountains, an upper-floor home with windows that overlook the all-encompassing city skyline or an adobe residence which is facing to the sunset in the desert, the majority effect of wow is bound to be created automatically. All you need to do is to enhance the appeal with the right facilities and the right design. Of course, anyone is aware of the wow factor, but it is usually accompanied by the cost of. Therefore, let's consider cultivating the wow factor through an excursion to the mall and then doing some decorating and renovating--a less expensive option than putting for a cinema.

Here are a few ways to make your space pop without having to pay for front-row seats at nature's shows:

Take a picture of large, vibrant artwork and hang it in the front entryway or in the foyer. The purpose of the placement is to create a stunning initial impression. It doesn't have to be a multimillion-dollar Jackson Pollock. Just find something large strong, striking, and fits with the color and style of your home decor. If you're not a fan for art, talk to someone who does. A professional artist or interior designer acquaintance will surely have helpful suggestions for what will work with what.

An alternative that is subtle: create an atmosphere of "enchantment" that is evident when the first day of entering. Put down a charming or funny welcome mat or give your space the name you want and then put the name on a sign made of wood at the entrance to your home.

* Make sure to remember the guidelines for captions which we will cover in step 3. Pretty Pictures: You may choose to identify the specific rooms that guests are staying in. Choose something similar to"Moonlight" for example, or"Moonlight" room if you have a great view, or "Moonlight" area if it has skylights that offer a spectacular view of the stars as well as "The Emerald City" if the interior decor is green. The name should be related to the theme of the house or the design for the space. Make it fun and creative! If you're seeking an artistic feel it's the ideal option to

give your space the personality it deserves. Because Palm Springs has a celebrity past One of the houses is home to "Liz Taylor,"" "Sophia Loren,"" "Audrey Hepburn" as well as "Marilyn Monroe" bedrooms. Along with"James Dean" bar "James Dean" bar. The entire space pays homage to these stars with massive artistic representations of the stars that evoke emotion.

If possible put the lawn with some artwork so that you are able to draw the attention of guests before they even enter your door. Animal sculptures made of metal, colorful wind chimes, festive decorations such as statues or flags, outdoor hanging lights--there's a vast variety of options with each of them suited to conveying an individual impression. Free and eclectic, or elegant and professional, you can do some research on the Internet to decide on the look you'd like to convey. Websites such as Pinterest.com are great for identifying ways to include tiny details that make an enormous impact.

* Wayfair and Houzz are excellent online resources for decorating ideas for your home and ideas for decorating your home. Airbnb

itself. Look through other peoples' listings to get ideas.

You can also check local real estate publications to find luxury properties and Architectural Digest, Dwell, Coastal Living, and Veranda magazines. For inspiration from the mid-century I'm a huge fan of the magazine Atomic Ranch. There are no limits to what you can do with it.

Another important aspect to consider prior to creating a stunning space is to consider the style you'd like to portray. If you're planning on making renovations and decorations yourself it's best to choose a style you are familiar with. My home is on my home in the New England beachside, and I've lived across the country, which has provided me the ability to adapt to various styles and moods. Consider what people expect from guests when they visit the location you're thinking of.

Also take into consideration your market. Are you considering buying property in an area popular for its chic shopping area? Perhaps you are interested in a charming spot that is popular for bachelorette parties? Consider the type of people who could be drawn to this place.

***

Here's a true tale that can help explain the details and nuances that go into the procedure. It began with my desire to move in Palm Springs. I am a huge fan of Palm Springs, always have. I purchased my home just before Airbnb became popular and revolutionized the way we book hotels to stay for vacations. When I boughtthe house, I was worried about where I would be going to stay and how I would be able create a home that would feel like my home. It was difficult to commit to the property without an outdoor pool. In Palm Springs, having a pool is almost a legal condition for building. However, I fell attracted to the house when I first saw it and it was comparable than a tiny apartment than a traditional house. The gardens were lush as well as an airy and spacious feeling of space inside and an overall style that was in perfect harmony to my style.

While I was settling in my new home, I began to realize the potential of Palm Springs as a tourist location and the possibility of owning a rental vacation. That led me to give the area an opportunity to build another home (with an outdoor pool) which would be slightly more suitable for guests. I soon realized that while it was a struggle at times, I was enjoying designing the house to entertain guests and offer guests a memorable trip. In the end, I was renting out the primary residence home as well! The absence of a pool wasn't as big of a problem as I had hoped.

If you have the right mindset and a good marketing strategy, you can create spaces that are attractive, even if they initially seem not the best for many guests. The presentation is all about spin it!

As these things go, my ideal setup wasn't going to last forever. Palm Springs put forth a referendum to prohibit the rental of vacation homes. The previous season, the town introduced new and strict restrictions and rules. It was the perfect time to broaden my options and diversify my vacation rental portfolio. First places that caught my eye was Paso Robles, a beautiful city located in the wine region located on the California's Central Coast. I had previously lived there for a period of about three years therefore I had a solid idea of the area's geography, as well as its potential as a tourist attraction.

However, there were some challenges to overcome. Can I earn a profit from an area with a higher property expense as compared to Palm Springs? Can I find reliable housekeepers? How do I find a home that was quiet enough to isolate my guests from neighbors as well as their family members? Can I find a house that would meet these needs but still be close enough to shops and dining establishments to allow guests to take advantage of the kind of things that people like to enjoy at Paso Robles? The central part of the town was home to a couple of beautiful homes for sale at affordable costs, but their proximity to neighbors seemed like living in a community. There were also many large, more affordable homes situated on the outskirts but they were far from the city's culture and nightlife. They could be reached only by dirt roads. There was also a lack of service for cell phones as an issue within the Boondocks. This is a major one. The first of a myriad of issues guests might encounter due to the absence of cell service could be the inability to locate the location on their smartphone's GPS. It's possible to have purchased an entire collection of scenarios that could be a nightmare.

While these worries rumbled in my mind, I decided to take a step back and assess the situation. I set off on a series of tours around local properties to experience them myself and to get a feel for their potential. As an agent for real estate I was cognizant of the importance of their time. precious, so I adhered to the traditional rule of making inquiries only. I also narrowed the search to online prior to the tour and restricted it to the top potential buyers. If I could locate the perfect property, I wanted to purchase as soon as I could.

Then, in Paso Robles, that was much easier said than done. If the cost and distance to downtown was right the view that led to the home was sad. There were times when the route involved homes with cars parked on the block or through industrial areas. This is not a great beginning to a vacation and especially when they're planning to travel through wine country. This should be kept in mind while searching for your dream properties. It's not just about place, location and what you need to do to get there. Another factor that was a hindrance was the existence of peaceful suburban homes for families. It's not the best location for bachelorette parties or wine-tippsy limousine-loads of partygoers.

Do not attempt to fit the rental of a vacation home into an area filled with families! The result will be angry neighbors, unhappy guests, and plenty of hassles for you.

I was getting anxious; my search was not yielding any results. This is also a one of the challenges: finding homes that you don't love can be just as beneficial as finding the perfect location. You're developing your perception as host and coming to know what you like and do not like about your home. All of these abilities develop over time, both conscious and in a non-conscious way. Keep an eye on the location, condition, population as well as the vibrations of transportation. You'll sense the vibes and get a sixth sense of the things that could go well. When you finally discover a dream home, you'll be able to ensure that you're not missing any vital aspects and that it's an ideal and not an unrealized nightmare.

I chose to focus on a specific section of the city to narrow my search: the West Side. This area of town was home to lots of vacation rentals and second homes as opposed to family homes that were primary and was located near downtown. When financing started falling in place, I conducted some quick searches and found three properties that were just put to the market.

One: A multifamily located exactly downtown. As I explored the property, I discovered the layout was odd There was not much daylight inside which created an unsettling, dark environment. In addition the next house was a shabby old sofa that was on its front patio. I try to look beyond the current decor and imagine the possibilities of what a space can become. My preference is always undertaking improvements and then having the satisfaction of an improved end product. To get the best quality meat, you must begin with good bones. This was a shambles due to design.

#2: A complete fixer-upper situated just outside of the city's central area. The reasonable price meant I'd have plenty of money to put into renovations and repairs, however the amount of money I had in the budget would have altered it from the reality that I had a carwash right across the street, and an water equipment warehouse adjacent to the property.

Uncontrollable factors which would totally destroy the wine-drinking experience desired by those who rent at Paso Robles. Next.

#3: A stunning home in the hills, just a bit away from the town square yet still near to the city. It was a quick drive or long walk to the shops and restaurants It was a lovely drive. Victorian homes dotted the California hillsides, and wide-open ranches dotted the areas of gold grass which faded into lushly green deciduous trees. This was the kind of thing people talk about when they speak of wine country. It's not an eye-sore.

The house was on a cul-de-sac that was small, so traffic was a bit less. The houses around it I observed, however, had important details that reflected their position as second, not family homes: there were no basketball courts on the driveway, or swings. These little details are an obvious indicator that these properties could be empty for long periods of time. Perfect. The interior was also than perfect. It had wow factor throughout. The windows in the wall let in a large view of trees. The terraced property of the house meant that, whereas the front entry was on an elevation of the street, its rear was sloping down and was adorned with plants and trees which gave a vast and stunning view. And the trees were large gorgeous California oaks.

It was evident that significant upgrades and renovations had just been completed, and were done in a stylish and elegant manner. High-quality wood, stone lighting fixtures, it covered all the way from good workmanship. There's no way to be perfect, but it's a good thing. The house was advertised as a three-bedroom but it was actually a three-bedroom located downstairs (realty codes is "basement") and shared it with a brightly lit laundry room. It was not perfect. The upper living area was huge. The entire home was used as the media room. I thought that this could be better. What if I placed the TV in the living area, then and then walled off the media room for a bedroom and then polished down the downstairs area by walling off the laundry space and changing the ceiling light bulbs in order to transform it into an enjoyable bedroom? This would result in a four-bedroom residence instead of two bedroom home with an unfinished basement sleeping space. This all sounded fantastic.

But . . .

There's not a twist-end here. This was my dream home. I purchased it. Even though it wasn't perfect I was able to discern the differences between fixable and not fixable issues. The bones were strong. The location was great. I could see certain improvements that could be made and even made allowances in my budget for these. However, if I had resisted the house due to some flaws that I may have let a fantastic property fall out of my control.

***

Every aspect of this stage--from location, utilities to maintenance, interior decor, the natural surroundings, and even deal-breakers to imagining the future, must be considered in order in order to make your guests' experience at Airbnb worth the time and effort.

Here are some things to keep in mind in your home search:

* Seasonality

What time of the season will your home be the most appealing to visitors? It could be different for each location. If you live in Vermont the fall season could bring tourists looking for to see the changes of color in trees. If you're considering an area in Tahoe What is the best way to understand how the traffic in summer be different from that of winter? In summertime, you'll be able to see gamblers, boaters, and hikers. The winter may also include the snowboard crowd, which tends to tend to be younger.

What kind of weather does your home get all year round? It might be in the ideal spot to get warm by sunlight in summer, however how will the light change in winter, when the sun is higher than the sky?

Do not forget the additional cost of de-icing or snow removal as well as frozen pipes that living in colder areas is a requirement.

How can you improve your use of the facility throughout the year? Find ways to attract the types of travellers who may be in summer, spring autumn, winter too.

* Guest numbers

Consider the local laws and regulations as well as any restrictions from HOAs, neighbors etc. prior to making any estimates.

If you take these factors into consideration How many guests can you comfortably accommodate in your space? Can an additional room be converted to an additional bedroom? Is a common space suitable the possibility of a sleeper sofa? What are the bathrooms available? Are there smaller things such as space for dining, cabinets for dishes, or seating on the sofa?

* Rates

Do you want to get the most of your money without putting off guests by imposing prices. Does your house fit the budget that your guests be spending on their accommodation? Urbanites will be drawn to the rooftop penthouses and those on a tight budget may be looking for ways to save money with style and feel that resembles a hostel.

* Parking

Are there driveways or garage, carport and street parking? What number of cars can be accommodated in the parking space? Are there parking facilities nearby? What time limits are in place? What time does the meter need been fed? Would you be able to recommend a great parking space within a block or two?

* Desirable features

You can highlight your property's top features. Pools, views, granite countertops, hardwood floors, proximity to local attractions--remember to highlight advantages and make them prominent in your online listing.

***

Be sure to consider the finer details. There are plenty of possibilities for things to fail. I found a fantastic house to buy in a completely distinct location (and state) which I felt at ease traveling to and loved living in. I was thrilled when my proposal was accepted! The house I was looking for met all my requirements very effortlessly. It was a distance from the neighbors and was quite private. The city was able to permit rentals with the abbreviated and somewhat loose short-term rental regulations. The house was not surrounded by houses that had the swing set or basketball hoops. No multiple parked 4x4 pickup trucks. No cars on the block. No hanging laundry. Just a gaggle of mid-century-modern and mid-century-traditional houses. Actually, the house was previously an accommodation for vacations. However, at the time, I wasn't thinking to inquire about whether the prior owner decided to sell prior to signing an agreement to purchase.

When the offer was accepted, and shortly before I had to transfer the earnest cash the money, a shocking "disclosure" was made public. It was apparent that the neighbour across the road had previously was a tyrant, bullied, or threatened guests at the property. It was such a bad situation that the holiday rental agency was forced to transfer guests to different properties they manage at least once. What are the possible comments? Yikes! The owner brought the neighbor to court and obtained the restraining order as well as a judgement. Right after the restraining order, the neighbor had put up some type of anti-short-term-rental signs on his property. A vigilante neighbor who is crazy is a deal breaker. Thankfully, this story brought it to me prior to when I had even begun the deal.

In Palm Springs, I later was told a similar horror story of neighbors who would shout at families who were playing at the swimming pool "Quiet!

That's no way to be this the Holiday Inn!" That owner of a vacation rental was soon gone. Even if the rental is permitted in the city and the location and home appear perfect, something could be lurking that could ruin your business idea. Do your homework and research!

Chapter 2: Innovative Programs

The vacation rental property you own will be an investment. You want it to appear beautiful for photos on the website and you'd like it to impress guests when they walk through the threshold. Consider this: photos of your home are bound to appear everywhere on the people's Instagram and Facebook accounts. They'll share with their friends the incredible spot they discovered and the wonderful vacation they enjoyed on their trip. The appearance of a property is extremely crucial when it comes to Airbnb. Airbnb game. If you're the first to decide to buy a specific home to host guests, it's the perfect time to think about how to dress the property up.

"It's an advantage that beauty is skin deepor else I'd be sick to the core"

--Phyllis Diller

The first thing to consider is what are the "bones" that make up the house. What's the layout? Are there open spaces and windows which let the space breathe? Are there narrow corridors and rooms that are narrow with a small size that you'll need to minimize? Imagine how many can comfortably stay in the space without stepping on one another's toes.

Improvements happen gradually. When you become familiar with the area and get feedback from your friends, decorators or contractors, it's possible to have a an idea of what's feasible within the walls. It will take some time to figure out the things that are working in the space and not working. Perhaps that breakfast area is located in a stunning spot near an open window covered with drapes of sheer curtains and the sun is shining through them right at the eye level, around 9 a.m. It's not something you've thought about this, but it's the perfect time to consider the installation of venetian blinds. Perhaps the chairs that you've set up around the table in the living room are perfect for the décor however, since they're an packed with stuff, guests will have to walk a bit to place down (or more importantly, take out) their beverages.

Research your local market and find out what Airbnb listings are available in your area. rent the most depending on the amount of reviews they receive and the frequency. Review the reviews that are both negative and positive. This will help you understand what's important to you in your neighborhood. Floaties for your pool are an advantage. Kitchens that don't have a lot of cooking equipment aren't ideal. What is the standard color palette? What accessories are common to be wearing? What's the "look" that is appropriate for your location?

***

A lot of these things will show up with time and use however, others can be predicted and designed to be planned. There was a time when I purchased a property which could be considered an improvement, even though it was it was not a major one. It required significant cosmetic enhancements but not massive structural or systemic changes.

My funds were stretched quite long to get this done. The challenge of securing a sufficient down payment and conserving enough funds to be eligible for loans was massive hill to climb. As I've told acquaintances I was cutting up pennies and looking through couch cushions to find change in order to help me get the numbers to work. Once I could afford the property I had to come up with a new way to spend my money.

My budget was set to focus on basic things, such as refinishing floors, painting and sprucing up the exterior of the house, re-doing the fireplace and so on. Beyond that, I required to furnish the space with furniture. After all these expenses, I ended up with little or no cash to spend on other purchases. One of the main problems I had to overlook was that the pool had to be replastered and didn't have the essentials of a heater for the pool. The plaster, though ugly and flaky, was not the most significant issue. It wasn't even an issue of structural nature and was not hindering the enjoyment of enjoying the pool. I was hoping to have guests enthused enough by the home's design and the interior that by time they arrived at the pool, as my theory was that they'd be willing to overlook flaking plaster. (It proved that my cost-saving plan here was right in that for nearly the entire time, was not one complaint concerning the flaking plaster!)

However, the heater was an additional problem. The absence of heat in a pool is not a good idea for winter swimming, particularly for those who are hoping to enjoy a warm Palm Springs vacation no matter the season. Although many people believe that California is sunny and warm all year round, the reality is that it can get cooler and so does the water. The pool must be at least 84 degrees in order to be safe for swimming. Guests expect and deserve the best comfort. Therefore, as when it became economically feasible, I decided to install an electric heater for the pool.

It's a lot easier said than done. Remember that I'd poured everything I had into repairing the basic issues. The house was then taken to the market with no heater. In my Airbnb profile, I was sure to state that a heater was in the near future however at present there wasn't any. So, I began accepting reservations in March. Even though the weather was a requirement for an outdoor heater to maintain an unarctic temperature for swimming but the house was to fill up. Since the cash flow from these rentals the business associate and me set aside money and then used the money to put in the heater!

***

The moral Don't be embarrassed when you find your home missing. Be transparent and truthful in your description of your vacation rental and conversations with visitors. If you're looking to begin renting, but you have a problem that's not yet addressed, comply with the three steps to acknowledge that there's an issue, discuss the issue by talking to guests (offer discounts, additional amenities, or another method of compensation) and immediately, if you can, act to correct the situation.

Admit. Address. Act.

If you're understanding and diplomatic regarding the issue--which obviously you should be and no business owner has ever been frustrated and angered by their customers. Potential customers usually give the ice. Keep in mind that you can offset your weaknesses with other advantages such as features, benefits, or particular considerations. This case is an example of the advantage of self-management, and is one of the benefits of Airbnb's platform that is open. A vacation rental agency could not have gotten my business without the heater, whether in March or in any other month. Of course, even the agency that granted an exception and accepted the listing, they would have received an 80% cut. It's a win-win circumstance. Instead of being forced to live in accordance with the rules of someone else's I could be flexible and list the property in any way and be able to meet the demands of guests using other methods, including discounts on the financial side. Self-management requires patience, perseverance and knowledge however the rewards--and profit--are definitely worth it.

***

I've shared with you my first home that I lived in in Palm Springs, the one without a pool. It's a pity to be without a pool. thing to do in the scorching heat in Palm Springs. However, just as the absence of a heater in the pool did not stop me from renting my second home in winter I'm not frightened by the absence of the pool.

Here's what I did to compensate with the luxury of a pool. This could have put off some guests concerned about frying in the scorching desert temperatures. In exchange for their willingness to give up a relaxing dip, I promoted the property as a bargain deal. With the help of the fact that I bought the property at a bargain price, I promoted the property at the price of a single-bedroom apartment for the entire home. It turned out to be an attractive proposition and the lack of a swimming pool or pool being a problem.

Actually, this approach led me to a completely new market I didn't even consider. Many people don't visit Palm Springs for a pure holiday filled with relaxing in the sun and relaxing swims. There are many business people and staff members who travel to Palm Springs for the numerous events, such as for the Coachella Music Festival, as well as its vibrant art and food scene. Additionally families with a tight budget would like to visit Palm Springs too, and when they have lots of relatives and children and relatives, they may not be capable of affording a home which is large enough and has pools.

Business travelers, those who are just passing through, or people travelling for other reasons than pure enjoyment and fun - these are all potential guests waiting to be discovered. Make sure to think outside the box when you're considering possibilities for your home and choosing a strategy for marketing. Although I didn't have as many rental properties during the summer, my rental income from this house increased my savings to the point that eventually, I was able to have that pool. In the end, with the construction of a new pool the revenue from the house increased by a significant amount. The house was a step towards the success it had already achieved! Particularly in the long run being open to specific markets could be more profitable and beneficial than you think.

***

There is no requirement that everything be perfect in your space initially. It is important to highlight its strengths Naturally. Take, for example, the property that didn't have a pool heater: We wanted to accentuate other facts-- like the mature fruit trees around a mid-century-modern-house in Palm Springs--and, to go with the orange, grapefruit, and lime trees we were providing access to a fruit picker. (This is a device used for taking fruits off trees and not a human.) To complete the process we purchased a basic juicer (not an extravagant model). It is now possible for guests to choose fresh fruits straight out of the trees. They could create healthy and delicious juices. Juices can be used as mixers later on in the daytime. This all fits in perfectly with what is known as the Southern California experience, and it helped keep the trees trimmed. Everyone is a winner!

This entire process is a continuous process and you are able to alter your plan as the state that your savings accounts are in alters. It's important to be aware of the improvements and future improvements you'd like to achieve and to strive towards the goals you have set. It's not only big-ticket items that can result in huge increases in revenue. Things as simple as improving the quality of your photos or adding an work of artwork to your walls (don't ignore Pretty Pictures and the importance of the WOW factor) will catch the guests' eyeballs on Airbnb.com and increase your rent rates. Consider these cost-effective upgrades to make up for any shortcomings in the home.

One of the most fundamental and obvious principles of flipping houses is to keep your expenses lower to ensure that when you sell your property at more expensive prices and make a profit, you can maximize your profits. When you are making Innovative Improvements for a vacation rental investment property, it is best to follow this advice and. Make the best of cosmetic improvements, but stay clear of bigger construction projects when you are able to. Also, put lipstick on that pig and it could become the ultimate cash cow.

This doesn't mean you are able to atone for any aspect of your property, or that you ought to look to reduce costs by letting the most important aspects slide. Certain aspects of renting out vacation homes can't be sacrificed. If you do not adhere to any of these rules and you fail to adhere to these rules, nothing Pretty Pictures, discounts, or quick fixes can wash the bad taste from your guests' mouths and your review and earnings will suffer the consequences. Don't let these issues go unnoticed. Here's a list of the non-negotiable aspects.

This could serve as a list of essential items you'll need to be aware of, in order to cover everything from common sense.

Essential Maintenance

* Cleanliness

Broken appliances or plumbing fixtures

* Toilets that are dirty

* Do not allow this to take place. It's a given.

* Water leaks

* Staining carpets

* Pillowcases or bedsheets that are yellowing

• Get rid of them and ensure that all your bedding is lily-white.

* Furniture that is rubbed

* Window spots and collecting flies on the sills

* Dead houseplants

* Termite, Ant, rats, or other pests

* This is especially crucial--imagine that a guest is looking at the cockroach. There are many people who freak out over these kinds of things, and with the right reason. Your star rating is gone on Airbnb.com.

Do not forget about the outdoors too. A swarm of wasps settling in your backyard could cause a guest to lose their entire vacation.

* Any unfortunate odors

* Observe dead or unclean trees or plants in your yard

* Pruning, weeding, watering, and fertilizing are vital for houses that have gardens. Employ a gardener if have to, and make sure you include

this in the cost estimates upfront while looking around a property.

* Food that is old or rotting stored in the refrigerator. Check that the condiments and long-lasting fridge products aren't also.

* Basic Hotel Facilities

* Unreliability of hot water

* Roofs with leaky roofs

* Poor insulation or poor airflow

In the event that your visitors are boiling hot all the summer, they'll quickly forget what they experienced. They'll keep it in their minds. No pun intended.

* Safety

* Smoke alarm batteries

* Refresh them at least once per year. I usually do this on New Year's Eve, which is easy to remember and also it kicks the year off with peace of mind.

* Fire pits and fireplaces

Keep in mind that fire and guests shouldn't be mixed!

Sometimes, you're unable to be without one, like in the case of a ski lodge for example. However, fireplaces can be dangers that are huge.

* If you have a fireplace in your house and you're looking to ensure it's just decorative (a good idea) Make sure you remove your gas lines. It will be able to serve as a lovely design without putting anyone in danger.

Also, unless explicitly stated or advertised the guests are not allowed to use fires of any nature. There are exceptions for, like a beach house which opens to the sand and has open brick or steel fire pits. (Even in that case, you may prefer to not allow it to minimize the noise from outside.) However, generally speaking you shouldn't allow guests to be arousing pyromaniacs.

* Stoves

If you're using gas burners, ensure that there aren't any leaks and the ignition mechanism is working for every dial. If it doesn't, it's making a request for a gas valve to remain open.

* Oil spills or toxic chemicals on the driveway or garage

Take a look the underside of the kitchen and bathroom sinks and think about the contents under them. It's best to avoid your guest's child to get into the poisonous bottle.

* Pest traps

Think about any rodent or insect poisons you've thrown out. Did you get every single individual trap? If you're not vigilant it could lead to catastrophe if the guest's pet happens to stumble upon any of them. It's also an unpleasant reminder that your house could be infested by something.

* Electrical problems

* Are there any exposed wiring? Are there any outlets that have burn marks? Unusual smells? Electrical problems must be resolved promptly. In the event of a delay, you could end up awakened to receive a notification about an injury to a guest or your home burning down.

* Unsafe decks

Lack of railings damaged by termites or fungal decay or unstable supports all could be dangerous.

* Floors with imperfections

Inequal surfaces or thresholds for doors that are high or weak areas could cause the toes to rub, or even more serious.

* Slippery stairs

* Your freshly oiled and polished hardwood stairs might appear great, but make sure to install carpet runners or alternative form of grip to keep from falling and slips. A laminated sign will also keep guests on the handrails.

* Showers and slippery tubs

Make sure you use the correct handles and grips for your floors on all bathroom surfaces. It can also be a big assistance to older residents who have trouble to get in or out of the bathtub or getting onto or off of the toilet. The majority of accidents in the home are in bathrooms, and also on the staircases.

* Furniture that isn't stable

• Fix the wobbly legs of your chair. This could lead to accidents more quickly than you think.

* Carbon monoxide leaks

A odorless, invisible killer. Find a detector and get your property inspected.

* Radon

As with the previous point do your best to not bombard the guests you invite to your home with particles of alpha. Check your basement for Radon.

* Other contaminants

* Black mold, asbestos and lead paint - the list is endless. A professional is required to determine the status of your home's property regarding these concerns.

After you've dealt with the fundamentals of cleanliness, safety and ease of use, it's time to think about more aesthetic aspects--things which give your space character and make your stay unforgettable. There's more to improving the property other than spending money and hoping for stunning results. You shouldn't be able to hand all of these tasks to contractors and interior decorators regardless of what your budget. These experts, though definitely skilled craftsmen and adept at their job however, they do not possess the broad-view that you have. Your view of all changes is from the perspective of your vision for the future as well as your marketing strategy and your ideal clientele. You're able to always share this strategy to your friends and family, but be aware that if you don't put your efforts as the final supervisor, your changes could not work exactly as you had envisioned. There's much you can't modify about your home however, you can increase the positives and lessen the negative.

In the step 1, Fantastic Finds, the location of your property can be an enormous boost to the appeal of your home, or be disadvantage that must be dealt with. Also, it is really hard to know how visitors will respond to a house because everyone has their own notion regarding the terms "convenient," "quiet," "safe," "comfortable," and "not infested with snakes" refer to. I know however, you'll never be in a position to please all. However, if you put on an effort to anticipate the needs of your guests, you'll avoid some of the ranting that occurs in Airbnb.com reviews and comments.

Here are a few easy and effective ways to take the pressure off your eyes and ear-sores

and Sound. and Sound

Fencing and hedges can provide an architectural and visual protection from all kinds of challenges. They protect dogs as well as basketballs that are errant from the neighborhood youngsters and parents as well. They are a good way to deter burglaries (though you'll need to stay from securing your home by using barbed wire or chain links). They can also reduce noise from the street and can be an issue in particular when your home is located close to a major highway or in a city that is crowded or in close proximity to bars and restaurants.

* Curtains that block out light and sound serve the same purposeof blocking sound and light, at the discretion of guests. If they'd like to get up to the dawn, no problem! If they'd like to lay down off the hangover until noon, no problem! They're less likely awakened by the shining sun or the garbage truck arriving at 6 a.m. Curtains with blackouts are also a great option in rooms with large televisions. Blocking city light and street lights at night by using thick silk curtains will give your living space an ethereal feeling. When your system for entertainment has become among your main selling points, think about creating a cinematic atmosphere.

Soundproof windows and insulation -- same as mentioned above. The guests will only be aware that an area isn't properly soundproofed. It makes paying for such improvements an effort that isn't worth it, but equally important.

Aside from that making bright, well-lit and cheery spaces can to alleviate any concerns about the view or location. If people are attracted by the light that is coming into the interior of a gorgeous space it is unlikely that they will take enough notice of the view out. In addition, people naturally gravitate towards vibrant colours and patterns. Make use of imaginative paint schemes, art furniture, cool furniture, and quirky decor to ensure that they are focused on indoors.

* In spaces in which blackout curtains are not appropriate, such as the kitchen, for instance-- sheer curtains will keep out the glare (and any eyesores outside) but still let through enough sunlight to lighten an area.

Pictures of kitchens that are bright and with counters that are lined with fresh food is an Instagram "lifestyle" essential. Explore the internet for ideas and soon you'll have photos of your house appearing on the hashtags.

One great way to think about guests' needs is to try a few tests at your home. It should be enjoyable! Let the space be available to your family and friends for a few minutes and then see how they react. You can even plan an "working holiday" and spend the night there. When you and your guests notice that you're slipping on the floor, falling on the floor or banging your head against an unattractive cabinet there are some potential improvement ideas on your list right away. Understanding the actuality of living in the home is vital. It's easy to see beautiful things in pictures however, in actual life uncomfortable furnishings angles, toe-stubbing obstructions and too-long power cords are quickly apparent.

***

We've all been there at some point or other I once was tasked with entertaining a bunch of family members over a full week. Her family and my sisters were visiting town and it was my responsibility to me to ensure they were able to meet their needs and they had a fantastic time. So I thought I'd get two birds in one stone. I put their accommodations for them at no cost on the ranch-style wine country property but with the condition that they give the property a trial run and inform me about any issues that were not addressed. Everyone gets to win!

Then, at the end of the week my sister brought a problem to my attention that had not ever crossed my mind. She said that it was extremely annoying that the bathroom did not have an magnifying mirror. This made it a lot more difficult apply makeup routine in the morning. Particularly, she'd thought of wishing she had a stand-alone and moveable mirror could be moved to the bedroom to perform her makeup regimen while husband washes. This type of feedback is always very helpful. For someone who doesn't wear makeup, these details didn't come to my mind.

***

It's only one small part of the many that make vacations pleasant and easy. If my sister had thought of something I hadn't anticipated What kind of comments could I have gotten from an elderly grandpa? (Bigger message on welcome cards, with the door's number.) Single mom with a 2-year-old? (Plastic protectors for electric outlets.) A gang of teens and their stressed parents? (A simple remote control to turn to turn on the television and not let the children from getting bored.) Businesspersons traveling by themselves? (An iron and an ironing board to ensure their clothes aren't wrinkled.) The variety of guests' needs is as varied like the guest themselves. There are likely to be needs that differ based on age, gender, relationship, parental status, as well as many more. Another reason to get to know your customers, gain familiar with their preferences, and be prepared for every aspect you are able to.

***

Every now and then it happens that something jumps out of your body before the guest starts their stay. Each time, I experience the feeling that I've forgotten to finish my homework. I'm irritated and feeling a bit frightened. What that actually signifies is that I have the chance to fix it before anyone notices. Some time ago I had a client scheduled to rent one of my Palm Springs properties in the winter. The property was complete with a the pool (newly heated!) with fully-equipped kitchen and a barbecue, the space was ready for guests to enjoy an amazing week filled with delicious meals and exploring the town's contemporary and trendy vibe. Our conversations on Airbnb.com prior to my visit revealed the possibility that he was especially attracted to the barbecue. In fact the guest didn't even inquire about the kitchen or pool in any way. This guy is a griller. He'll likely spend longer standing on the Weber rather than cooking on the stovetop in the kitchen. Then I realized: I'd never put in an outdoor lighting system to light the barbecue. At this time of the season, it was getting dark by the time dinner was served. Thankfully, there was about a month to go before his lease began. I installed a beautiful lighting fixture, which I utilized during guests' stays. When that guest walked in I pointed it out to him and mentioned his passion for grilling. He was delighted and I behaved as if it had all along.

***

Pets

Another type of customer could offer a variety of wants and needs that you may find it difficult to anticipate. They'll also never leave an Airbnb review or even to be able to speak with the person about their experiences. Pets, when you allow them to stay, pose an interesting challenge. Here are a few tips that can help you make your residence more pet-friendly (and pet-stain-resistant).

When a dog-friendly guest has had a stay, I've developed an exclusive method of identifying any unnoticed "accidents." My method is to combat fire with fire. I let my puppy, Reggie, in and let him explore. If he's seen a flurry to the curtains that are floor-length it's a very likely that the guest's dog behaved like an hydrant for fire. This trick is perfect to clean up stains. Also, as a pet, Reggie gets a kick of all the scents. If there is a sign of an accident then dip the edges of the curtains in an empty bucket of soap as well as warm water. In other places Nature's Miracle Odor Remover is a great solution. It is also believed to deter pets from contaminating the same space in the future.

If the pet-friendly aspect is a major feature of your home think about using vinyl or other surfaces that can be washed instead of fabric when you can. The reasons are simple. (Not to mentionthat you'll be protected if your guests are expecting a child or spill the contents of a glasses of wine.) The most vulnerable areas you may want to think about using vinyl include the mentioned curtains as well as bed headboards as well as chairs and couches, and everything else that's at the dog's level.

Cats aren't as popular in the realm of animal companions for travel, however, if you are attending the Cat Fancy convention is in your city, you might want to provide an empty litter box and a new litter bag. (Personally should I ever be you asked me, I wouldn't permit a cat to stay with me, not because I don't like them , but because I own one.) Cats don't just scratch furniture, but they are also likely to flee the premises and could even get lost.

Labels and signs

If we're thinking of the ideals of guests' satisfaction and ease and comfort, the struggle to locate essential items or a rising feeling of discontent with the intricacy of a gadget aren't the first thoughts that spring to your mind. Visitors aren't at your house to repeat all the issues--disorganized closets, the tangled remote for your TV or the frigid shower faucet they've dealt with at home. If there's something wrong in your kitchen cabinetry, plumbing or television, something along these lines, keep in mind the three letters: Admit. Address. Act. Inform your guests about these nagging areas prior to time. Make sure that you're solving the issue. One effective way to do this is to clearly label the areas of confusion, and then providing clear, easy-to-read instructions to guide the issue resolved. Make sure you take action to correct these issues ahead of time whenever possible.

If the Blu-Ray player won't play when the TV is set to something other than Input-4 for instance, or the glass sliding door is unable to close unless you raise it with the handle an inch and you aren't able to fix these issues prior to the rental date then it's time to take open the labels. Make use of something more durable than an ordinary Post-It and write your message with something that is more legible than Sharpies. If your handwriting is a mess, scratchy, you might want to print labels or instructions sheets in the most appealing font. Labels can serve as guides for dealing with a difficult device, or for navigating complex digital tech, warnings for children and pets or as a quick method to ensure people can locate what they need.

You might want to label areas such as:

* Closet shelves

* You can dedicate a labeled shelf for every size of bedding linens (full King, queen etc.). You can mark which towels are suitable for on the beaches and what ones ones are intended for bathing. Label the laundry hampers as Clean and Dirty or Colors and Whites. The specifics depend on the configuration of your laundry room. Try to look at everything as someone who has never had the opportunity to use the facilities you offer previously.

* Trash

* Recycling, composting, landfill? Make sense of any confusion by using the colorful labels.

* What time is the day that the trash goes out? What is the best place to put it? What can or cannot be picked up from the trash truck?

* Technology

Instruction sheets are essential for the operation of many of the complex technology that runs through our world. Provide guests with a printed guide for Wi-Fi network names , passwords, and instructions on how to set your television to connect with cable to stream movies or video games, and so on. What do you think of surround sound? Find out how to use the air conditioning thermostat and the controls for pool or Jacuzzi heating. Alarm systems? Sprinklers? Kids-friendly Internet filters? Smart (or especially stupid) appliances? Coffeemaker? (That one's crucial.) Garage doors? Take a look at all the elements listed and think about what features of them might frighten guests.

* Kitchen

Have any of these microwaves which requires eight buttons to nuke something for 30 seconds? Note it down. Does your oven take an extended time to heat? Which is the silverware drawer? What are wine glass holders? An inexpensive labeling device can work wonders.

* Bathroom

* We hope that you do not have the issue however, if your toilet requires some extra focus to flush properly it is a good idea to put an inscription or sign--"Jiggle the handle" or any

other technique you'd like to use. This is a nagging issue which needs to be fixed quickly!

Set up a warning sign that will ensure that your guests don't flush feminine products in the toilet. Tampons can cause a plethora of clogs to the plumbing system. You can later read about how I learned this painful way.

* A shower that is too hot or cold could be a scathing experience. Many people hate fiddling with knobs to achieve the correct temperature while they are freezing in the tub. shower guidelines are a huge advantage if their functioning isn't clear.

* Windows

* Latch broken? Take note of that specific window isn't opening. If windows are closed for security reasons, make certain to inform guests of this as well. It is also possible to mark windows that are sticky by writing "Please be sure to open carefully"--broken glass can be something to avoid.

* Rules and rules and

Include a printed copy of the rules. Noise ordinances, guest limits, pet policies, water use restrictions--whether these kinds of things are imposed by the host, the city, or common decency, make sure to spell them out clearly. This will give guests an idea of what is expected and provide you with a solid foundation for you to defend yourself in possible dispute.

A crucial point to remember when you own the pool: there should be no glass on the pool! It is important to ensure that your guests use plastic objects only. You should also provide plastic and paper plates and utensils, margarita glasses and so on. To ensure compliance.

The instructions should be are numbered and as simple and easy to understand as is possible. Include co-host and host contact details, details about your house, such as Wi-Fi passwords and gate codes as well as emergency numbers for local emergencies. Laminating instructions sheets is a good idea, it costs just pennies to do this and the plastic also makes them more difficult to tear, spill onto or even lose. It is also possible to put them in areas that are more humid, such as near the sink or inside the shower.

I make use of a tiny and affordable Dymo label maker to provide thorough instructions. The labels are able to stick to virtually every surface, and are perfect for marking small items such as remote controls. In the vicinity of staircases and steps I prefer to place adorable little signs. On the top and bottom of a staircase the signs I use say "Please Pay Attention to Your Steps and Stay on your Rail!" I also frame the signs I hang on the toilet that exhort users not to flush the tampons. (Seriously should they flush them it will have devastating consequences.) There are a variety of affordable, elegant and stylish frames in Michael's or other retailers that are easy to mount on the wall using only one nail. It's worthwhile and adds an authentic B&B style to your home.

Room Setup

The ambience of the bedroom will affect guests' perception of their stay. As the name implies the most important aspect of the room is its bed. Make sure you choose it with care. Size or location, the level of comfort and bedding can determine the appeal of your living space.

It's not fun to squeeze yourself and their belongings into a space with a bed that's too large for the area of the floor. The guests will appreciate space to move around and breathe more than they would be able to do with a bed that is one size bigger than it needs to be. It's important to ensure that the bed is in line to the floor plan as well as the furniture. If the room can technically be suited to a king size bed however a queen bed allows greater floor space, think about the smaller size. Perhaps it's more beneficial to place one twin bed on each side of a room instead of one large bed in the middle in the space.

There are a lot of factors to think about: is this a family-friendly vacation rental? If yes, then two twins make more sense for younger siblings. If there is already a bedroom with two twins, perhaps you should consider the full size bed for a second bedroom. You could also connect two twin beds to create a king. In reality, a product known as a wedge or bridge is made to achieve this. It's not the most user-friendly however the benefit is that beds can be separated when needed. Adults may choose to utilize twin beds too particularly for small groups of friends that don't have any couples or bachelorette parties. Consider all the choices and the many combinations that different types of guests could require.

Always have a writing space or desk in every bedroom, if it is possible.

There are many business travelers who can make great use of a workspace or even if your guests are on vacation and want a space to set up their laptops or recharge their devices. I'm also a big fan of having luggage racks that fold up for guests to put their bags on. It's an easy and small addition which is greatly appreciated.

Bunk beds aren't recommended. They're only suitable for children and, even if kids do enjoy them they could pose security issues is too high to justify them.

Decorating

The first step is to identify your weaknesses. It could be having excessive knickknacks or little. Once you've organized a room, ask an objective friend make additions and subtracts according to the need. I've noticed that I am too minimalist. In contrast, many people I know are trying to squeeze too much in a room. A lot of tchotchkes can create an atmosphere that is cluttered and could overwhelm guests. A lack of them could make your home appear unclean, similar to an office or a hospital. There's a delicate balance to strike in this area. External recommendations can be extremely helpful.

If you're struggling to decide about (interior as well as exterior) decorating ideas , and everything else fails, duplicate the style you love. Check out magazines, Airbnb and vacation rental websites, Pinterest, or Martha Stewart. There are plenty of suggestions that are available.

At first, the exterior of my home was dark green and I was certain that I wanted to paint it lighter in color. The home was, let's put it this way: ugly. That was the main reason why it was being sold and the reason I bought it at an affordable cost. I was thinking of going with white, but which shade of white? What about accents such as the trim and front door? I drove around almost every road within Palm Springs looking at mid-century houses to discover the perfect shade scheme. When I finally found it my business partner an architect, took the Pantone colour chart (when it seemed like no one was at home) in daylight to find the exact hues. Our house is now beautifully decorated and beautifully decorated. Inspiration is available almost everywhere.

Picture and TV Position

When hanging a photo that is hung, make sure it's centered horizontally to the average eyeline. If you're 5'8" or more and you're in the middle, ensure you're in the middle of your image is aligned with your eyes. If you're taller, squat down. If you're less tall, ask someone taller to assist you, or take a measurement of the distance of 63" across the middle of the wall. It is advisable to find someone with an excellent feeling of equilibrium to assist you in the selection. Pictures that are hung too high will make the room appear crowded because the visual effect makes the ceiling appear higher than it actually is. Pictures that are hung too low can create the illusion of an old dollhouse, and not in a positive way.

Based on Houzz (which we are in agreement with) The majority of couch seating heights are around 18 inches above the floor. For an adult, the eye height sitting in a comfortable manner is around 24 inches higher than the seat. The ideal central-of-television-height for a typical person sitting in the range of 42 inches (18 inches plus 24 inches).

https://www.houzz.com/ideabooks/47203714/list/how-high-should-your-tv-be

Decor

The ability to anticipate the needs of your guests and arranging everything in the space in a well organized manner shows your guests that you truly are concerned about their comfort and pleasure. Art pieces or ornamental elements such as objects or simple knickknacks are best suited, as with all other things, to give the room a complete "feel." Be sure to pay special focus on things like color schemes as well as the style of the decorations. The house is designed an experience for guests. It must reflect the locale and the natural or cultural setting of the area. The design elements must be chosen to create a feeling that guests are they're experiencing an experience, such as experiencing the "Colorado" feel.

Vegas ought to have an "Old Vegas" feel. Do not make it about the style of your house. It will be more appreciated by guests if you have an environment that visually appealing and matches the location. If you live located in Utah or Arizona, you can decorate your home with Red Rocks of Arizona or Utah and Utah, you should play up photos of the artwork of Zion National Forest and clay colored accent walls. Do not put up Union Jacks on the desert area regardless of whether your an Anglophile. The area you choose to decorate should match the one that you reside in. Navajo blankets work well in the Southwest and not for New England, just as lighthouse designs would be unnatural to be seen in New Mexico. The theme is determined by your location. It's pretty simple. Don't be too concerned about it.

More guidelines on the environment:

A room that is Miami-styled would include a number of watery pastels with a sense of nightlife, beachiness and relaxed living.

* The "log log cabin" experience will consist of wood exposed plaids, camping-inspired elements such as Thermoses, furs, warm blankets, as well as the general rough-hewn look of a survivalist. (Even the most luxurious comforts of home is provided There are plenty of ways to create the illusion that you are "roughing it.")A Southwestern adobe would include clay earthenware pots, objects, some vaguely spiritual sculptures and mysterious art pieces such as Kokopellis, Navajo or Mexican blankets, a terracotta tile roof and a palette that includes dusty desert reds and oranges.

*The New York high-rise experience would consist of lots of glass, modern furniture of black leather, chrome or stainless steel, and contemporary art on the walls. Cultural features such as framed jazz LPs, or famous posters could further define the mood.

But, be careful not to get carried away with this one. It's not necessary to keep everything totally in line with the themes. You can include neutral, or even non-neutral components that mix and function together. This is known as an eclectic style and it's what differentiates professionals from those at the corner store.

Don't fret. Style is a matter of practice and you'll get to this style in time.

The most important thing is to stay clear of the sloppy or boring, as well as the outdated.

If you've thought of the appearance of your home and its conveniences your guests are sure be amazed. They'll be impressed by the love you have for your home and the opportunity it offers for them to sit back and enjoy the surroundings you've designed for them. Perhaps you own a beach home that is full of boats, ships and lighthouses. It also has the Southwestern-printing chair which sits beautifully in a corner of your room. Let's say that the room includes a mid-century, earthenware lamp that is placed next to the chair and has similar color to the print of the chair. These various pieces can tie together, giving your room an authentic look.

It is important to realize that taste involves space, color, selection as well as other compositional elements and not just money.

The choices you make need not be costly to look stylish. If you're on a tight budget do not rule out auctions, garage sales or consignment centres for amazing furniture and art. Goodwill or Salvation Army, or even the local moving sale are full of items that may cost a penny however, they look much higher priced. Finding some of the latest and trendy objects is a great option to fill up your space and make it appear "lived in" and conveying a specific style and saving money.

Books for the coffee table are a cheap method of instantly filling the mind of guests with specific meanings. Even if it's not possible to decorate your living space to look like an music lover or art collector A few carefully placed coffee table books about the subject (wine in Napa for instance) can make a big difference in convincing guests that they're getting authentic experience.

Decor is the final product of your decorating process. Decor is important to show off on the form of Pretty Pictures and should also offer maximum comfort as well as being sturdy and easy to clean. Consider all of these ideas into consideration when picking the colors and accessories to decorate your home. Be aware of the requirements for all types of gatherings such as family, comfort as well as work and leisure. One excellent (though somewhat outdated, excuse the look of the late 1990s) resource is Martha Stewart's How to Decorate. It covers the features needed to meet the various needs (comfort and work, etc.)) along with strategies to break down a home into its components such as lighting, windows, floors, and walls. There are a myriad of design ideas available. Take a look, research, and browse some examples, and figure out what will work to your house.

Visit our "Dear Airby" section on our website.

(www.masterofvacationrentals.com) and submit design questions so we can reply with ideas or example vacation-rental listings.

Chapter 3: Pretty Pictures

The perfecting of how you present your Airbnb.com Profile is by far the first step to ensuring that you get the amount and quality of guests you're hoping to attract. Anyone who hosts you will be able to find you on the website, so creating the right impression on guests is crucial. Prospective guests would like to discover their dream holiday spot, whether it's a cozy cabin located in the countryside, a stylishly furnished loft located in the middle of the city or even a beautiful beach house. It's up to you ensure that the pictures of your property appear as attractive as the perfect Instagram lifestyle photo. This means thatwhen making and selecting pictures, it is essential to put in the time to prepare, pay focus on the details and emphasising your property's top features.

The Shots You Need

Smartphones can capture photographs with a resolution which is superior to the professional cameras that were just two years back. You can make use of your smartphone to take photos, but ensure that the photos are properly lit, artistically designed, and clear. Poorly composed photos make it appear suspicious that you've hidden something. They also convey the impression that you're unprofessional.

There are a few tips to keep in mind while you're taking photos of your home.

For instance:

Be aware of the lighting in your room. More light is better But make sure your images aren't too bright and muddy. Also, avoid images with too dark colors. Make sure that the images are well-lit. If your photos appear a little dark, but look great it's simple to alter the brightness by using the settings of your smartphone. You can also transfer the image to your computer and edit it by using the built-in functions which will already be installed.

* Make sure that your images are focused! Highlight all the cool elements of the room with high-quality details.

Kneel down in order to take images so that the room appears as if from the viewpoint of a sitting person instead of standing. Keep the camera parallel to the floor, at 90 degrees-- flush the object of interest. Try be wary of the tilt downward many beginners choose to take pictures. The most damaging photos are those which are taken in haste from the typical "a person who is standing to take pictures" angle.

Take note of the balance and composition of the image. Take large sections of the wall or spaces on side of image. You can do the same cropping if you have lots of floor or ceiling visible. It is okay to show some floor space above furniture, but not too much. The idea of splitting the photograph horizontally into three thirds and placing the main focus in the middle part of photography is known as"the "rule of Thirds."

* Do not include multiple photos of the same space from various angles. It's better to feature only one strong shot instead of many weaker shots.

• If your photojournalist or you are planning to process images using Photoshop Be sure to be realistic. Images that have been processed and highly filtered can make things look unnatural.

The panoramic function of the camera in your phone can be utilized in moderation to achieve the effect of a wide angle of a room. However, ensure that the result doesn't cause the room to appear blurred. It can give visitors the impression that you're not representing your home and trying to turn the space appear as if isn't.

"Pour yourself a glass of water wear some lipstick and get yourself back together"

--Elizabeth Taylor

If your phone's photos don't look great and you don't own an expensive DSLR (digital single-lens reflex) camera, think about hiring an experienced photographer. It's possible to search Craigslist or, even better locate a local estate agent whose pictures you like. Ask their manager (as you offer an honest thank you) to see if the manager would be willing to share the contact details of the photographer. Be prepared to shell out a few dollars of money to get truly outstanding photographs. For those with a tight budget, student or amateur photographers may be able to provide the photos you want. Make sure to look through their portfolios, and make sure they're able photograph indoors. Make sure you choose the best quality and aesthetics that are featured in magazines that are geared towards the design of your decor or home You want the photographer to be able to make your home look as attractive and appealing as is possible.

There's a third option as well. Airbnb can arrange for you to have photographers for a small fee. The only downside is that it could take a long time to make an appointment, and during that time you'll miss important bookings.

An Airbnb photographer could be a great way to supplement your pictures, however, you'll have to get the first batch of photos taken care of by yourself.

https://www.airbnb.com/professional_photogr aphy

The art of telling a story

Think about how you will present your home in both images and captions. Don't be smug about your property. If you don't like your home, then and neither will anyone else! (Harsh yet true.)

Imagine taking a potential guest to a tour around your property. What are some unique aspects you'd like to display? Create a scene in the mind of the viewer. Create a sensory picture of the preparation of an exquisite meal or having a enjoyable dinner with your people you know. Create a caption that includes action words. "Cook your way through a feast in modern and stylish, well equipped cooking area!" Name the bedrooms and then think about picking themes for each. Enjoy it, and show that you are a person who is genuinely happy in your home. You can be straightforward or complex. Choose them based on the color scheme, or the style of the art or another theme. For example: "The Haven bedroom features ample sunlight as well as a luxurious queen size bed and French doors that open to the patio."

The pictures should be updated whenever adjustments and modifications are implemented to the house. The guests should already know your home by looking at the photos. If there are significant differences that they'll be unsure why the photos aren't up-to-date. If the house is clearly different from the images it could be that they be disappointed.

More Detailled Images

My property is equipped with a gas barbecue in the outdoor space. It's a nice feature that is attractive to guests. I believed it was evident in the photo of the patio, however one person asked me if I had one. I realized that I had only made reference to that grill within the caption and it wasn't apparent in the photo. Following this I was sure to include it inside the descriptive text and then I changed the photo of the patio to show the grill in a more prominent manner.

When people inquire about certain items, it means that the answer isn't immediately obvious. If this is the case, you'll need to modify your image, your picture caption and listing description so that it is evident what type of facilities you're offering. Sometimes, guests might inquire about an item you don't possess. If it's readily available inform them that they can get it and after that, take the item in hand and bring it to the home prior to when they arrive. As an example, a customer recently asked for serving platters. I knew that the home did have one, but it required more. We introduced a variety of forms, colors, and styles of serving equipment to the home, with mention in the description on the internet. This simple change was made across all our properties.

Spicing-up Your Listing

Make sure your captions for photos are engaging! The worst thing than not having any photo captions is having captions that only contain adjectives within the description. Include many adjectives and verbs to give a vivid picture of the house!

Embellishment--instead of "Large outdoor patio with BBQ" add "Enjoy the western sunset view from the patio with seating for 10 guests and charcoal grill."

The most important summary of one house reads:

Take a trip to wine country with this modern and cozy four-bedroom architectural mid-century California-style ranch home on two-thirds an acres. It's part-tree house, and part ranch-style. It's situated on a tranquil West Side street and a quite wooded lot, yet it's .7 miles away from downtown! A car ride of four minutes or a 14-minute walk. It's the closest thing to the rural feel you can find in the downtown area. Be aware when walking down the hill towards downtown that it's uphill when you come back :)

A short description, but nonetheless full of details to aid the reader in understanding the location. The book is a tale of the dream of living in the woods and living on a vast lot surrounded by trees and deer, while enjoying the most modern amenities that civilization can provide with the close proximity of downtown. Visitors can imagine enjoying the sunset, and then walking into town to enjoy the night. The scene has already been painted in their heads. They are able to envision the way their vacation could unfold, and it looks fantastic.

"Freshen the appearance of" the listing each 30-60 days to benefit from the latest and enhanced feature that Airbnb provides to make your listing show up in search results. It's a good opportunity to add new information or create a appealing image in your visitors mind, and make sure you're in the top position of results for searches.

Chapter 4: How To Locate The Ideal Region To

Start

If you do not own a house it is best to determine some of the most suitable areas to move in. There are numerous options to consider which area you'd like to select. The most important thing is that if are planning to live in the house regularly, you could be more drawn to the perfect place to reside in for a portion of the time or even spend your holidays in.

If you do it is possible to sacrifice regarding things like accessibility as well as the amount of rental opportunities per year , and the kind of people who are attracted to your business.

It's a crossroads. While I usually focus on finding locations that can generate income, you could belong more to the category of looking for an area to relax or even live.

Also, we must consider that buying or establishing the rental of a vacation home away from our main home will result to the difficulty of running the vacation rental from a distance.

Whatever way you choose in, you'll need to find the right compromise between what's most likely to be best for you and your preferences.

One of the items I think of first when I am considering expanding into a new area are listings of vacation rentals .

It's a simple method to determine if an area has enough number of customers to be useful. For instance, you could extremely easily use Homeaway, VRBO, and Airbnb to find an area you believe could be a good getaway rental spot.

When I look through the list, I make note of.

How many vacation homes are there?

This can give you a good idea of the amount of demand in the region. If you can see a massive number of holiday rentals, you'll be able to feel confident that there is lots of interest. But what it does mean is that you'll need to compete to get those reservations however, don't worry about it now. Consider these tips and then we'll determine what market that you could participate in.

What types of vacation rentals are your primary options?

Are the winners mostly bigger homes such as cottages, condos, or condominiums, or are they a mix of both?

If your location has diverse terrain, you'll want to look into various holiday rentals until you find the right type of accommodation that best fits your budget and income to get to the ideal spot.

Location

In keeping in mind the style of house, let's examine the location of each. Are there more people who are booking properties closer to downtown?

Are you near a theme park or along the beach? Learn about the theme and you'll be able to determine where you'll need to be. Do not think that you have to be in that particular area otherwise you'll be a failure.

While location is crucial in the choice of holiday rental properties, amenities, and price are also highly rated.

There's a possibility that you're out of the zone but possess sufficient amenities and characteristics that other homes don't have, you might be able to draw the attention of potential buyers.

Amenities

Are there any amenities that you simply won't in a position to live without? For instance in Florida near Disneyland almost every house has a swimming pool. Are you sure you'll be capable of securing a lot of reservations if your property does not have the pool?

Perhaps, but with the possibility of a significant discount. We're not only seeking out the latest trends; we're also seeking out possible niches. There was no one in my neighborhood providing a huge open space to play in, a room, or even a bath tub. So I set it my mission to offer the same and distinguish myself from other people.

Do not just consider the actions of others. Always think outside of the box when it comes to opportunities to stand out from the crowd. Similar to the Hotel Amenities Arm race in which hotels competed to draw customers in with their facilities.

If you're located near an lake or ocean or a lake, having a set surfboards or paddleboards for your guests could be appealing and what do you feel about cruiser bikes? There are many alternatives available to attract people to your house.

Reserves in the amount of

How many reservations are these properties getting? Particularly, what appears to be the most popular season, and what is believed to be the lowest season? What is the duration of each season. How dramatically do rates fluctuate based according to the seasons?

This is crucial to determine whether this area will be your financial sweet spot. If it's not the right fit for your financial situation and you're not sure, there's no reason to invest in homes in this area. We'll talk about the best way to find your ideal price and what is a good fit financial wise later in my book.

Remember that due to season and the time you're looking at a specific area you might find that vacation rental properties do not have a lot of bookings. It could be because you're in an area that's so far outside of peak season that they've not yet received their reservations for the upcoming year yet. Be sure to check back with specific regions at certain times of the day to determine if reservations have been filled.

Furthermore, just because a listing shows reservations, it doesn't suggest that they're reservations. For instance, if you search at Homeaway or Airbnb you can check the calendar on the page and see dates that are marked red. This typically means the house is booked. But, it could also mean that the owner has blocked the dates because they'll use the house. This is why it is important to combine information from the most listings within the region.

* Demographic Research and Who you're looking for

What I like to do after going at the listing and coming across an extensive amount of information that reveals the kinds of homes, locations and income I am likely to see is do some research directly on the area to find out what kind of tourists are likely to be drawn to these areas.

We'll take Myrtle Beach and Miami as an illustration. If you go directly through Myrtle Beaches' website, I find that they describe the place as "Family and welcoming with plenty of family-friendly attractions". The best part is that they have their annual visitors listed at 14 million, which is an excellent number to keep in mind.

Similar to the Miami's site. First thing I notice right off beginning is that they state "From Miami nightclubs to bars and live DJs, a complete report on Miami dance nightlife."

From this little nugget we're beginning to get an approximate picture of who the general population is and who is likely to be drawn to these locations. Miami is likely to be a younger crowd looking for entertainment options, while Myrtle Beach will probably be bigger, older, and have children.

It's enough to say that it's not wise for us to only rely on an information resource. The next thing I'll usually do is go to city-data.com and enter the city and region.

For instance, Miami has a population of 200k, with on average, a 36-year old while Myrtle Beach has a population of 22,000 with an average of age 42. Therefore, my theory that Myrtle Beach attracting an older crowd is now receiving more evidence, as its median age significantly older than Miami.

While I'm still on the site , I went on the forums for the region and read what locals have to say about the region. It's also an excellent chance to ask them questions you have on your mind.

Next thing I'll do is use Nielsen Demographic Research https://segmentationsolutions.nielsen.com/my bestsegments/Default.jsp?ID=20&pageName=ZI P%2BCode%2BLookup

If the link isn't working then try a Google searching of Nielsen My best Segments and search at the tool for zip codes.

This is an excellent site to learn more information about Market Segmentation. For instance, if you visit the Nielson Demographic website you can choose to search for zip codes to find the demographics of people in the region or look up demographics based on.

This will tell you the areas where people are likely to reside across the country.

The reason behind taking this step is to discover the type of people living in particular regions.

Then, you can determine the kinds of shops and entertainment in the region.

Businesses are geared towards the local population. If my region is known for its younger active crowd,

I'm sure there's going to be nightlife and enjoyable events for the group.

This site is pretty thorough and dives into Psychographics which analyzes the demographics and delves into their minds: What television shows do they enjoy and what activities do they engage in to have enjoyment, food, the automobiles they drive, etc.

So, for instance using some of the information from the Miami zip code I found this population profile.

"29 American Dreams - psychographics include: going to the zoo, watching E! Entertainment, shopping at Kaiser and read Tribune ethnically, and different families."

So what this says is that it is possible to count on the region to be home to lots of diversity in culture because of a wide family composition, and people are obviously interested in pop culture based on what they read and watch and so I can anticipate nightspots and hip scenes.

It sounds like a spot that could be an ideal attraction for younger millennials and for those who enjoy the best of culture.

This site is among my favorite sites for diving into the thinking of demographics. It is an extremely powerful tool available to you. I have spent hours delving into the psychology of the various populations in specific areas.

Your best target Market

I think that families are among the most easy areas to concentrate on in relation to Vacation Rentals.

The reason is that their requirements aren't satisfied outside of vacation rentals.

For instance families will typically require a lot of outdoor space. Most homes are designed or could be designed to allow for that.

The majority of families want to to cook a full meal. It is a great fit into the specific niche that vacation rentals offer. Families wish to have a space that is spacious and the most up-to-date entertainment space.

This can also be easy to accommodate, since most families do not wish to share their facilities with their neighbors. In addition, they're only staying with the people they like.

Additionally If you end up having a home that is large enough to be intended for multiple families you can guess what they're likely to do? Divide the cost of the entire home that means you'll be able offer a more expensive rate, but they'll be paying less than a hotel , and receiving more, in a way.

According to surveys conducted by travel experts There are more than 1.5billion leisure trips being conducted in the USA by itself, and more than 70 percent of them are family-friendly and 40 percent are multi-generational. That means grandparents as well as their grandchildren are all gathered in one place.

Does this sound like something you could use for rental properties on vacation? Yes, and that appears to be a huge market.

It doesn't mean I would suggest that you limit your expansion to areas that can see an enormous influx of family members as this is also contingent on how you intend to manage it.

Your home is a place to be. For instance, family members who travel to your home will definitely be searching to rent the entire house. It is possible that you are focused on renting a spare room. My small cottage has performed very well at the pursuit of single travelers as well as young couples who are traveling around the town.

Take the knowledge you can gather from these suggestions wherever you want. Remember that whatever style you're experiencing for the area is what you'll build your home around.

The Area is awash with events The Area

As of now, I have an idea of the seasons, housing prices, demographics, and seasons. If I'm still in love with the region, I'll look for more specifics of the area that draw in tourists.

To do this I'm looking for the most sought-after shopping areas themed golf courses, parks, beaches, parks, etc. In reality, anything I believe would fit into my own demographics and prove for the reason why homes in particular areas are receiving more requests.

In addition, I'm also interested in seeing whether the city has any national popular events. For instance, Ashland Oregon is known for its nine-month Elizabethan theatre program. Austin Texas has a giant music festival; and some cities host Ironman events. These types of events could be huge boost for the market of vacation rentals and could increase rents significantly due to these.

City-data.com Forums, HomeAway, Airbnb, Vrbo the official website for the city, and, of course Google are all good choices to locate these types of events.

Regulations

In the end, you should never to sign up to any region which has strict regulations for vacation rentals. As the popularity of the sector, it's likely that it will be in a expansion phase. At some point , I believe that both the cities and vacation rental companies will come to a compromise that they can agree on. Some cities are making laws that limit the number days you are able to rent to ninety or sixty days per year. If I were you, I'd examine in depth the exact nature of what they're enforcing , and whether it's worth the effort on your part to look into starting a rental in the region. For the majority of people, it isn't worth it in the event that you're severely restricting the days of occupancy.

The most efficient method to find out local rules and laws regarding rental properties is to contact the city's town hall and inquire.

Additional Tools for Regional Data

One cool website is AIRDNA. They've scanned and collate all AIRBNB reservations and listings within the same area every year. The most useful thing about this is that you could purchase the AIRBNB map of a specific city and receive details such as the median listing price as well as the average number of booking days, the location of these houses, and so on.

You may even get separate data that shows how much you can earn for a four-bedroom home in comparison to a single bedroom home.

The information is quite extensive and will cost you. To me, more information you have, the more valuable.

Remember, it's only Airbnb information. It is still advisable on your part to study your

Homeaway as well as Vrbo listings to get more accurate information about your area. In addition in the event that your location isn't awash on Airbnb and Vrbo, you'll discover that the information can be a little skewed and incorrect. For instance, in my town it's much heavier on Homeaway listings than Airbnb, which means the data isn't as precise as it could be.

Their website can be found at

AIRDNA.com

* Housing Research

If I'm looking for a home that is available, I've done some research on the area and discovered enough evidence to convince that this is an ideal location for a rental vacation. The next step is to find the perfect home in the perfect location and, more important, at a cost that we can afford , and is close to our ideal spot.

The apps and websites I like using are well-known and function exactly as they ought to. Zillow or Trulia are great options to stay up-to-date with the latest listings in real estate in certain areas. These apps, you can make contact with reliable agents in the area that can provide you with updates on new listings that meet your requirements.

A word of caution Though I've succeeded in having the majority of my homes by myself, if you do choose to use an agent for real estate be aware that they are real estate agents and they're paid by commission.

It is crucial that regardless of the advice they give, you make your own judgments on the property they recommend. They're looking to earn money, and you're looking for the perfect home for your holiday rental. If they're trying to convince you to buy a house that doesn't make sense financially or isn't exactly what you're looking for you should just refuse. There are always more houses to find.

In this moment you'll be able to identify pretty close to the kind of people arriving in the area. You'll be aware of the size and what kind of house you'll require.

Be sure to follow your research and intuition regarding the house.

Choosing the Right Home

You think you've found your dream home, you're delighted and are eager to transform it into the holiday property you've been dreaming of. Before we sign the papers, let's take a moment and consider who will be using the property and why.

The top three reasons why people opt for vacation rentals is Location and Open Space and amenities.

Let's consider the first.

Location

If you've done your research, perhaps you've discovered a good location to build a home close to. What about the property itself? I'll tell you the story that is about the type of Condo located in the city scene. The description is:

"Amazing location in the downtown which is where the action takes place."

The sound is very great. But, there is one issue that is obvious, and that is that the bedroom of the condo is located right next to the sidewalk. It also features two large windows that allow anyone passing by to observe everything.

In addition the apartment was situated within the city's bustle and practically every night, in the early hours of the morning, you could be able to hear drunks jogging past those huge windows on the sidewalk.

Are you aware of how we're focusing on other people's experiences in your house? Now, I can say right now that the task of repairing a home that is close to a busy road and trying to create a more private space and, most importantly, peaceful so that people can get a restful night's sleep is a difficult task to achieve.

It is possible that you are only seeing positive aspects of the location of your house, but consider the potential disadvantages of a home's location. In the end, you'll be able to determine if the issues are fixable. Should they not be, then you'll need to determine the extent of a challenge this could cause your guests.

I've already talked about the possibility of noise from outside potentially being a problem. What other concerns could you imagine in relation to your guests staying at your house

Space

Another example is a house with a kitchen on the second floor , it's a rather odd layout that leaves much to be wanted.

If you're considering that you could be attracted by families, and especially multi-generational ones, do you think that the older members of the family will be happy to climb up and down stairs to reach the kitchen? Most likely not.

homes that have poor layout are difficult to fix and cost a lot to repair. People form their opinions about a property in the first 6 seconds of entering it. If you find a house that is poorly laid out is probably better to leave it alone, or talk to a professional and determine if it's financially feasible to address certain problems.

The most important thing to be aware of is that you'll have many guests in your home. Today people appreciate open spaces that allow to make it easy for them to move around the house.

Even if the house may possess some peculiar features to it, don't worry as you are able to be honest about it in the description for your listing. Be honest and identify any possible negative aspects of the property that could hinder certain guest experiences.

Consider the whole process of travel for your guests, from arrival to the departure. Where will they park? What is the best way to get into your house? Does the living space have enough space enough to accommodate the guests? What type of dining space and kitchen are you able to be able to accommodate?

The idea of thinking about these details early will ensure that you are with the ideal place for the right kinds of people.

Neighborhood

If possible, you should consider obtaining permission to stay at the house over the weekend to experience the area. Perhaps the home turns out to be great but how about the neighborhood? It might seem appealing right at the moment, but a stay-over for a few days can provide a better understanding about the kind of community you're entering.

While evaluating the area, you'll need to understand what your neighbors think of holiday rentals. The most effective way to get your rental property banned is to get complaints from your neighbors. You might be contemplating buying your dream home but find yourself stuck with one of your neighbors who is very stubborn against renting out vacation homes.

For all my holiday rentals, I try my best to create certain rules for my guests to ensure they are aware of not to disturb neighbors.

The range of options includes parking arrangements, non-noise hours, and even not going through their backyard.

Keep your neighborhoodand, most importantly , neighbors in mind. I'd even inquire for their opinion regarding vacation rentals and inform them that you're planning to start one and that you are a fan of their peace and desire to collaborate with them to ensure that they feel at home.

I've had wonderful neighbors in my time and I believe a large part of it is due to my ability to talk with the people around me about this. I provide them with my contact number and tell them that if guests are disruptive, blocking their parking space or trying to annoy them, to call or text me to have ended the behavior.

Sometimes, just letting your neighbors know you are there is an important step in maintaining respect for each other's home and space.

What is the best time to Shop for Rentals for Vacation Rentals

When is the ideal moment to start looking for rentals on vacation? The majority of the time, the best time to spend looking for a house will be in the non-seasonal times. The reasons for this are numerous. For starters when you're buying the property that's already used as a holiday rental, the chances are that they won't want to sell in the high season.

This means that in the low season , you'll experience a huge surge in rental vacation homes throughout the area. This means that you'll be able to choose of which one is the best for you.

The second reason is that you shouldn't to purchase during the middle of high-season. If you do then you'll probably be required to honor any bookings they make and not be able to earn this income for yourself.

Three, purchasing during the off-season lets you have the time to get your home prepared for the next season and set the stage for earning income in the fastest duration.

There's a chance that you'll be lured to purchase a home during the summer, when kids aren't in school and many are planning to move. However, you'll have to contend with more buyers and more homes sold that result in a rise in prices for homes. There's no guarantee that you'll get a bargain, however you'll have to contend with greater competition.

When I first purchased my holiday home, I purchased it during between winter and spring which was our slow season. This allowed me to finish everything that required to do and also to get reservations into the coming season.

Chapter 5: Finances

Spend a few minutes take a moment, while I trust and believe on the advice that I will be giving you. I am not a financial professional The advice I'm going to offer is based upon my personal experiences of more than a decade in the field. It is your responsibility to speak with a mortgage broker or financial expert before taking any of the advice that are provided in this chapter. thank you for your time.

Finances, it's the most feared hurdle that blocks many of the progress we make within our daily lives.

Consider the trips you've decided to not take due to financial reasons or dream jobs and hobbies we decide not to pursue due to the fact that we're told that we can't make a profit from it. What about the businesses you've chosen not to begin.

It isn't necessary to be looked as a wall that prevents us from moving forward in our lives. Sometimes instead of stepping over the wall, we need to overcome it. The debt is broken into Fixed Costs and Variable Costs. Fixed cost is a term used to describe a long-term debt that is usually anticipated and is paid at a predetermined price. It isn't subject to fluctuation and is typically paid out each month or every year.

Even if you don't manage a business, you may have fixed costs currently, like rental or even you Netflix subscription.

Variable costs are usually temporary, but can be paid off quickly, and may fluctuate based on the amount of usage. For example, you could pay for your electric bill can't be paid in full. But, each month it may vary in cost according to the amount paid, as well as other costs that fluctuate or debt are often associated with credit card or car charges.

The cost of a vacation rental are broken up by the above definitions and we'll be able to more precisely determine on what the most effectively.

* Be aware of your Sweet Spot

In general, when making investments in the real estate market,, they tend to stick to the rule of 1%, which means that for every pound of money you invest in something, you must be able to make minimum 1% on that. For instance when you take out an amount of 100,000 in a mortgage, you need to ensure you will earn at minimum 1,000 per month which is an important aspect of investing understanding, however, it's really more ascribed to rentals for long periods of time.

I was looking to create one that was more akin to short-term rentals, so what I thought of is what I refer to as"the Sweet Spot. What this can provide you with is basically ensure that you have a profitable vacation rental, and is also able to provide plenty of time to utilize for yourself if you wish.

So, what's an ideal sweet spot? The sweet spot when you are able to break even for all expenses and have just an occupancy rate of 30. Therefore, to determine if we're in the sweet spot, you'll need to conduct an analysis of break-even. This is accomplished by writing down the expected fixed and variable costs and adding them to an annual or monthly amount so that we can determine our operating costs are.

Let's record and find out the cost of operations we are each year. I'll propose the possibility of a vacation rental this based on the estimated average price of a second house purchased in America that is currently at 180k.

* Mortgage + Insurance + Property Tax 18,000

* Products (toiletries and hot tub cleaners Cleaning agents, towels etc.) - 500

* Advertising (vrbo, HomeAway, website, Airbnb) - 2,885

* Utilities - - 4,200

* Maintenance and Lawn Maintenance - 5,00

* Internet + Cable Amazon Prime + Netflix - 1,920

* Annual Total = $32,505

It is likely that you will identify a few things in these figures.

One: your largest overhead can be due to your mortgage. Similar to any other brick and mortar enterprise it is the structure itself that is usually the most expensive expense.

It is therefore obvious that it's beneficial in evaluating your next home purchase to be sure that the monthly mortgage you pay for fits the expected cost of operations and your expected income.

Second: I didn't mention the cleaning costs of the crews. This is that you'll be charging your guests the cost. Therefore, it's not taken from your income and is simply siphoned over. Some hosts don't charge a cleaning cost and instead clean themselves. These hosts are people who suffer from fatigue as hosts and don't consider this as being a business. We don't want this, therefore, you'll likely charge your guests for cleaning up and avoid the effort of cleaning following your guests.

Going back to the numbers, we can quickly come to the conclusion that to get to my 30% occupancy I'd require an accommodation that would earn at minimum $295.00 each night however it's only for a tiny part of the time of.

That's a total of 110 days of the year for $295.00 you've paid for your entire year's mortgage as well as the expenses related to managing your vacation rental which means that the remaining days of the year will be a profit.

Also, keep in mind that the numbers mentioned above are just variables in the cost per year; my rental property is likely to not cost me five grand each year for maintenance, as well as five dollars for materials. It is possible to reduce your annual costs for the form of entertainment and cable through finding ways to cut costs. I'll provide suggestions for in future chapters.

I've found this figure to be ideal since the most travelled time in the calendar is summer and the typical summer time is about 90 days and puts your requirements exactly in line with the requirements of the world's travel season.

You'll probably get much more rental days than 90 days which means you'll have plenty opportunity to make money and that allows you to find ways to increase the value of your vacation rental so that it can fetch an even greater price and thus put yourself within a cyclical pattern of progress.

If you can cut down on your expenses now, you'll be able enhance your capacity to grow and make a profit later on as these numbers weren't just a figment of air. In fact, all numbers correspond to a 30 percent occupancy rate, which is the minimum required to achieve succeed.

At the time of writing, the average cost of a house that is listed as "Investment or vacation home" is $185,000, and buyers as per recent research expect to pay $200.00 per night to rent a vacation home.

If you decide to have a 20% deposit and have an average interest of about 5%, then add your break-even analysis for the rental of a vacation home then you'll find the conclusion that with only 110 days of vacation booked, you will be able cover the entire cost of your trip.

It's true that you'll most likely be paying more than $185,000 for your house However, this figure can be adjusted by recognizing that there's a good chance that you'll find a home for less than 200 dollars per night.

Additionally what's more, the appeal of the sweet spot of 30% is that it allows for only 90-110 days of the year, which is enough to stay profitable.

That means there are an additional day or two in the year you could still book in order to achieve profitability. This is why I aim for 30% in my numbers . It gives me to maximize my profit.

Cash on Cash Cap Rate, NOI, and more

Alongside knowing your sweet spot , several additional financial tools that you can use to ensure that you're buying the right kind of property is to determine the Cap Rate as well as Cash on Cash returns. do not worry, all of it will be explained shortly However, before beginning this type of analysis, we must begin by collecting some basic information.

What are the most important factors that help the value of a home increase as we conduct this research on vacation rentals, it's best to concentrate on these.

* Property Attributes: The number of bedrooms and square footage, as well as the location.

* Purchase Cost - What price are you planning to buy the house at and the estimated costs? Make sure you take into account any renovation and interior design cost.

* Financing Costs - What do you expect to borrow and what's the interest rate currently in place and closing cost?

"Income" - what type of income can you rationally determine for this home?

* Expenses - Now we'll want to deduct the expected costs of operation, "mortgage,utilities,supplies,insurance,landscaping,maintenance"

Net Operating Income, Cash Flow and Net Operating Profit

To figure out our Net Operating Income or NOI, you do this by taking your expected gross revenue - expected operational costs, so for example if you expect to make 50,000 gross revenue and have 10,000 of operational costs your NOI would be 40,000 or 50,000-10,000=40,000NOI.

Be aware that we don't include our Mortgage, or more commonly known Debt Services in the NOI. The reason being that certain real property analysis tools are based on the assumption that you have paid cash to purchase your property. So should we include the debt payment in our NOI, the figures could be biased toward one type of analysis. Because we do not include debt services in the NOI, we're taking an assumption that you paid cash in full for the property is being analyzed.

The reason is that it provides you with an overall return that you can anticipate on any property, regardless of each individual's personal financing choices, but don't fret however, as the majority of us will not be paying everything in cash for our house We also have an application called Cash Flow which is your NOI Debt Services. This will show you the real annual return on the property, after taking into account your mortgage as well as any other debts that you have paid over the duration of the.

For example, we have a NOI that is 40,000.. Debt Services of 12,000 annually which is equivalent to 1,000 per day = 28,000. Cash flow.

Once we have both those numbers, we can begin to use some of the tools that can provide us an excellent, concrete piece of information that will help us make home-buying decisions.

Capitalization Rate

It is the best measure of return for an investment property. The reason why is because it is totally independent of any financing for buyers and remember that number of Net Operating Income we have come up with? Now is the moment to show off.

When you have figured out your NOI , you'll then divide it by the cost of the property to arrive at an overall percentage, for that for instance, if you paid 265,000 to buy a home and expected a NOI of $45,000, you'd get an 16.9 percent yield on your money If you speak to most people would be extremely happy with such a return. For most people , anywhere close to 10% returns is usually a good investment possibility.

We're basically saying that for every dollar you deposit, you'll receive 16.9 percent back on your investment, which when compares to savings accounts or stock account provides excellent returns on your investment.

I'm not saying that your vacation home will be guaranteed to have 16% return, but you shouldn't be worried if it does not. If you're able to show positive cashflows of 10% or more, you're well placed to protect your home and the future. However, this calculation does not include the possibility of financing from buyers and so let's run an instrument that will assist you in calculating the return you can earn from financing.

Paying cash on returns

Therefore, if Capitalization Rate represents your return with no financing cash on cash is your return after financing. Think about home design, mortgage and remodeling costs, and all of them will be included into this calculation . That's the reason I prefer this figure the most.

For ease of understanding math, let's say that we have a cash flow of 30000 and our investment basis for our house is 100,000. This is the down payment, renovations furnishings, closing expenses. So our COR will be 30 percent.

30,000/100,000=30%

I ran these numbers to help to comprehend the maths behind the equation and how it is working, but don't expect returns of 30 percent, %... but when you do locate properties that have the returns you want, put the book down and buy it now.

For the majority of people, an increase of 10% or more is an investment that can be considered a good one.

* MORTGAGES

Perhaps the most significant obstacle that one will have to overcome when trying to get into the market is the main property of the home itself and one of them is getting it. If you already own the house you'll utilize, then you're fortunate. However, I'll discuss some options for those who do not. It's worth reading whether you have a home or not since it does give you options should you decide to attempt and buy a second vacation home. Let's discuss mortgages and the requirements.

There are some things you'll need to have set up before you start the mortgage portion of the home buying process. Prior to that,

Credit Check

Your credit score plays a significant aspect in the rate of interest you pay for your mortgage. In the event that you've got poor credit score, you'll get a greater interest rate, and you'll pay more for your home.

If your credit rating is badly damaged, you'll want to work on it for at least six to seven months before you can even be eligible for an mortgage. To check on your credit, I suggest going to annualcredireport.com, and they will give you the report from the three credit agencies Equifax, Experian, and Transunion

Affordability

In the next step, you'll need to determine the amount of home you are able to manage to. For the majority of people, going with a current loan such as an owner-occupied as well as investment, the lending agency will examine the ratio of your debt to income. What is your income relative to the loan amount. In general, they will not allow you to be eligible for loans that are more than 40% of monthly income. This means that the total amount of your monthly debt must not exceed 43 percent of your pretax gross income under the majority of loan programs.

Let's take an example. If you earn an annual income of 100,000, or 8,333 per month. 43% of your earnings is 3,583. That is the maximum amount credit card debt that lenders allow you to carry on a month-to-month basis.

There are a few strategies to overcome this. Most of the time when you've found an excellent lender, they will be able to tell you the tricks.

Down payment

If the above two steps are favorable You'll need to think of your down-payment plans. The majority of conventional loans require 20% down at a minimum, but some loans will require higher than others. There are certain exceptions. For instance, if you are an owner-occupied property, it is possible to take out an FHA loan, which will require 3percent down.

At first, this may appear as an opportunity. However, you'll be paying a more expensive monthly installment,

and will be paired with private mortgage insurance or PMI that generally ranges from 0.5 to 1percent of the amount of the loan. This means that on an average 100k loan, you'll pay an additional $83 per month or $1,000 per year for just 1percent extra cost.

Along with the PMI like we mentioned earlier and you'll have to pay a greater monthly mortgage payment, which could be anywhere from two to three hundred dollars per month more than if could just put 20 percent down. If you're planning to stay in the house for a long time, it's financially advantageous to have the 20 percent.

In the knowledge that not everyone will be able to make it to 20 percent, it's wise to do the math.

Find out the anticipated income you are able to reach so that you can find the ideal amount and then determine whether your home purchase would fall into that category regardless of the requirement for 20 percent down.

Let's discuss the different types of loans available and couple of innovative ones you can use to purchase the home you've always wanted.

Investment Loan

There's no doubt what you're planning to accomplish using the property with this title. You'll be seeking income The advantage to this will be if you're trying to qualify for the house, they'll conduct an Rent Analysis in the appraisal.

What this means is that it gives them an approximate estimate of how much you'll be able rent this home each month. And , guess what? You are able to apply 75% of that figure to earn a salary that means you'll reduce your debt to income ratio using only an estimation of rent.

If you are close to achieving their 45percent debt in income, the option of investing in a property could help you to get your debt-to-income ratio low enough to allow you to purchase a home you want.

Now , you might be telling your self, "Wow.. I could earn 60,000 on rent through an accommodation for vacations with 75% which could be the bonus cash I earn towards my income to debt ratio. ..." Unfortunately there is no rent analysis on rental properties for vacations. Instead, they do it through long-term rentals. Vacation Rentals as of now remain unregulated for them to be used as an estimation.

The benefit of choosing to use an investment title for your house is that you'll be able report every penny earned from the property, which means that if your holiday rental is doing well , this extra income can aid you in obtaining a second property in the near future.

In addition, when compared using a conventional loan or owner occupied loan where you'd be required to limit the number of days of rental you can have on your property per calendar the year is when you are able to let it out for as long as you'd like. That is essentially more money for you.

A few negatives: first the most important thing is that they're bound have an interest rate that is higher. It is typically one eighth of a percentage point higher than a traditional loan or owner-occupied. It means that you'll pay a less each month as in comparison to an owner-occupied.

Owner Occupied

Many of you who owned houses in the past have heard of this kind of loan it's the conventional loan. It typically comes with a lower interest rate than a traditional loan, and is very common in the lending industry. The typical procedures are required to qualify for the house, which is either 20 percent down, and 20% equity within the house of the price of purchase.

However, based on the date you're reading this, there could be occasions in the economy when you can buy under owner-occupied , you may be able to acquire it with no 20% down.

In that sense it is important to be reminded to make educated choices.

The mortgage of your home will mean that you'll be financially free without having to pay the 20% down payment to reduce the monthly mortgage payments?

Owner occupied or back to normal is definitely an ideal choice for those. But, things can become a bit more complicated when you are renting the home out. Legally, you're allowed to let the property "Owner Occupied" for a fraction of each calendar year.

If you choose to adhere to these guidelines, you will be losing the opportunity to earn extra money in addition to reporting the income on tax time, you'll only be able to declare the amount you have earned towards your earnings.

If you're considering this from a business perspective, you could think an investment loan is a good idea.

It could be a good as a better option. Rent analysis may be a better option. to aid in determining eligibility, you can declare all of your incomeand aren't restricted on the number of rental days or only pay a slight more expensive interest. But based on your location and the regulations of that region the situation could be different.

It is best to record your loan as owner-occupied. Some regions, such as San Francisco have recently been creating jurisdictions for vacation rentals. This includes only permitting owner-occupied homes to be utilized as vacation rentals, and not allowing second-homes also known as investment properties to be used for vacation rental.

What regulations they have on this issue, I don't know, but it might be beneficial for one to first look up details about your local laws to determine what type of loan is best suited to your needs.

Lease To Own or Owner's Contract

This was the choice I chose to go with the first time I purchased my first house in the early age of 19 and I chose it due to a variety of reasons. At the time, I was contemplating entering the business of renting out vacation homes, the real property market was in disarray. This was in 2007 and the whole discussion was about the bad loans given out and the fact that everyone was filing for foreclosure, and banks weren't offering loans, and they didn't.

This created an opportunity for an Owner/Rent to Own contract to be completed. What you're basically doing is locating owners who would like to sell their home and then signing that they will transfer the property over to you, for a predetermined duration of time. Rent is paid at a predetermined rate and a specific amount of the rent is used to fund the capital value of the property.

There are plenty of positive aspects to this choice.

A: It lets the purchase of a home when you may not get one through the bank. Owner-carries don't require banks. Instead, they're arranged by escrow firms, and they do not conduct an identity check or determine whether you're able to financial qualify for the house.

B: it permits you to begin paying off the house at a much faster rate than through the bank. In the case of my house I was paying off half of the capital of the house in every single payment. To further explain suppose I spoke to the owner of the house, and we agreed to buy his house for the price of 100,000. We also decided to make the monthly amount at one grand. Half of that amount (five hundred) would be used to purchase the home, and the homeowner would get the remaining portion (five hundred).

In the course of one year of paying I'll have paid off the house 6000 dollars, which is a difference of 200 to 194,000. This may not sound to be a lot but if I had to get a traditional loan, I would have paid down about a one-hundred dollars in the first year.

Now, through taking advantage of an owner carry, I'm able to settle the mortgage faster, which means that I'm increasing the value of the home and giving me an opportunity to be able to get a mortgage later on with the traditional loan.

C: it permits you to also begin earning income, which can help you get the house you want in the event of refinancing with an institution. The home you purchased as an owner's lease is technically in your name and any revenue you earn from it is yours to declare.

This means that you stand a better chances of being able to get an loan at the time. Additionally, you technically own the property, meaning you can now deductions to help you save the cost of tax preparation.

D: In the majority of owner contracts, you can create a home mortgage plan. For instance, in my case I was fortunate enough to find the owner owned the property free and clear. He was also willing to make the monthly installment that could financially benefit me and him until I was eligible to purchase the house.

It's not just creating what you're legally able to pay each month , but also what percentage of it you'd prefer to put toward the capitalization of the home.

These are the main reasons I signed an owner's contract for my first house. I didn't have the qualifications; no one could however, there were owners that were looking to sell their homes. Therefore, they were willing to sign an owner contract carry until they were paid.

Every owner's carry is going to differ and you could pay a higher interest rate, and the owner might require you to raise more cash at the start of the. The length of the contract could be just one year, unlike an ordinary loan, which can be flexible with the bank. Try to set it up in a way that it works to benefit both parties.

The most effective strategy for negotiations is to ensure that each party is in a win-win-win situation. If you're not sure you have the right approach with this, don't feel scared to ask someone with experience, like an attorney for real estate.

There are risks to everything but the most obvious risk one with Rent to Own Rent to Own home, aside from not being in a position to pay the rent and not being able to refinance the loan at the end of the lease. However, this doesn't necessarily mean that you'll lose your home; this is contingent on the property owner you made this deal with.

If you've made your payments punctually since the start of your contract there's an excellent chance that the person you're dealing with will be willing to prolong the term but not take the house away from you.

It's best to know the the possibilities. Don't forget that the fact that you signed an owner's contract doesn't mean that the property is yours. If you don't find the funds to refinance your loan before the expiration of the term then there's a good possibility that they will return the house. If you play your cards right, you'll be able to use an extremely creative method to buy a house.

Commercial

If you are considering pursuing this particular field Here are a few points to be aware of. One is that your DTI isn't often considered in the application process for this kinds of loans. Instead, they're focusing at your LTV or loan to value , which is how much value they see in the property you own. You could also get a loan that is greater than what the property's value is to fund improvements or expansion, furniture and furnishing. There are many possibilities for commercial loans.

Anything you do should produce earnings in addition to this, if you decide to take the loan via an institution, most likely they'll require a balloon payment to pay the remainder of the loan within 3 to five years.

It's unlikely that you'll have the money to be capable of repaying the loan completely in the end, and you'll probably be required to refinance your loan to finish the transaction.

If you think this is similar to an owner-contract carry are not wrong however you don't have to do any searching for an individual owner who would be willing to make this kind of deal. If you can secure the loan out of the reach of an institution, there's the possibility that it could be constructed as a standard loan in which you pay it off over 15-30 years, with the possibility of a higher rate of interest.

If you opt to obtain one from a bank, keep in mind that once the balloon payment is due, there will be more conditions on whether they'll be able to refinance the loan.

They might take into consideration the field your company operates in, and whether they are hesitant about the business at the moment. Did you have trouble being profitable? Or they might simply find that their portfolio is too many loans from the field, and then pull out.

In contrast to dealing with an owner who might not have as many restrictions when it's time to refinance or extend the term even if you're not eligible in the moment the bank is more likely to not take that action.

*   Commercial loans made through an institution will probably have the option of a

balloon payment that lasts from three to five years

* The relationship between income and debt is seldom considered

* Need greater than 30 percent down the property

* Must generate income.

* Has a significantly more expensive interest rate, often by more than a full %

A few residential lenders be able to comprehend the requirements for commercial loans, so you'll probably need to look for commercial lenders.

Co-ownership or Co-signors

Another alternative for those looking for ways to be eligible is to join an individual. What this does is reduce your debt by half and also provide two income sources. For many people who are in need of a second source of income, this is an acceptable alternative and will enable them to be eligible to purchase a home.

Naturally, you'll entering into the business with a co-partner, which could cause a variety of problems in the near future. However, it could bring about a variety of opportunities. It is crucial to be aware of who you choose to co-sign with how much each will share in terms of profits and who's part is responsible for making choices.

Do you want to have the same work environment or is one of you the sole partner? If you decide to do this it will also affect who will take the bigger portion. All of this talk is about both of you as well as your partner in business.

It's also crucial to realize that the co-signer will be paying the debt as you are, therefore should you default on the payment for your house,

the credit of your co-signor will be impacted just like yours will. The co-signer is likely to have trouble being able to obtain credit in the near future, since the term is already on his credit record.

Tenants In Common or Tenants In Common

There are two kinds of loans people can seek in TICs. They comprise Fractional loans and group loans.

A group loan is one where each member of the group is involved in the process of loaning and divides ownership percentages between the group. The lending institution will require everyone to sign the paperwork for this kind of investment.

A fractional TIC loans are the way that everyone can take out a construction loan according to their portion in the building. It is usually a difficult loan to obtain as the majority of those who opt for a TIC will end up using the option of group loans.

The primary benefit of using the option of a TIC generally is that you'll be sharing the total cost of the property. Starting from the moment you approve the loan through the initial phase of the project , to the likely administration of the vacation rental, it will also mean that you'll be split the profit. If you're not expecting massive returns and want to cut down on your workload, this could be an ideal choice.

Chapter 6: Marketing

* WHERE DO I LIST

The great thing about starting your vacation rental now is that for the vast part, the marketing aspect has been done for you. At the time of writing there are several significant players in the Vacation Rental market, which include HomeAway/VRBO and AirBnB.

I strongly suggest that you write a make a list of each of them. However, they're both advertising to slightly different groups that means you'll need to meet the needs of different people.

Let me go over these sites and discuss what to watch out for in the following. In the next section, the management aspect of this book I'll explore each of these sites for listing that will help you improve your home's performance for each of them.

HomeAway as well as VRBO (Vacation Rents by Owner)

They are both the parent companies of both. You'll be able to register on both using the same account and I've used these since I began my ownership of a vacation rental with huge satisfaction. The businesses were established in 2004, and they later bought VRBO in their group in. They currently have the largest list of vacation rental properties with more than one million available in more than the world in 190 countries.

I love listing my house in my HomeAway and VRBO websites. One of the amazing features they provide that will make managing your home more convenient is the ability to book online which allows all your guests to pay and sign to the terms of your contract online. There is also an auto-generated welcome or thank you messages and an amazing hospitality Application.

This application lets you create an automated Concierge sort, which helps manage your home's security from far distances which is much simpler. The application lets you provide directions to your home, directions to access your home, the local restaurant and other activities, as well as amenities inside your home , and directions on how to utilize the app.

The Hospitality Application has been huge in reducing the time spent and making it much easier control your house and also for your guests to understand how to use electronics in the house and discover activities to take part in in the surrounding area.

The best part is that when the next guest has paid and accepts your terms through the web, Homeaway automatically sends out invitations to the application on their phones, allowing them to download it and get ready for their trip and, in the end, streamline the entire process.

Homeaway has developed a great deal since the day I first began using HomeAway back in 2007. Homeaway's Hospitality Application at the period was more in line of

of making multiple messages or calls. Instead of making a booking online , I had to write an original copy of my contract, then mail it to every guest, and wait for them the contract back. After they had left I'd send them the damage deposit. This is especially important if you own multiple vacation properties or manage multiple vacation properties may be a little difficult.

In regards to the client base of HomeAway and VRBO generally, I've noticed those who book later approximately 3 - 6 months most times, it's generations X families, which is typically, people are 35 or more in the age range of 35+. If you have a bigger property and are looking to sell it, HOMEAWAY and VRBO brand are excellent websites to advertise on. They offer larger group bookings and usually for stays of three days up to one week in total.

They provide a variety of kinds of listing options: You can list your listing for free with a deduction of 5percent off every booking, or you can list with an Property Management company who will typically collect between 20-40 percent of your rental income but will manage everything on your behalf including listing descriptions and linen services, the mortgage payment interior design, screening and reservation of guests and photography, among others.

If you're looking for a complete non-hands-off method to managing your vacation rental, you have the alternative. But, you'll lose an enormous amount of money. The one I usually go for when using HomeAway as well as VRBO is their annual subscription priced at $349.00 with bookings online enabled as well as $499.00 without.

My advice is to sign up for Their Online Bookings allowed. You will not only save money every year but also your ranking score on their site (which results in higher rankings) will improve with it activated.

AIRBNB

It's another major player in the vacation rental market. It's relatively new. It was established at the end of 2007 as Brian Chesky couldn't afford the cost of renting the loft he was living in San Francisco loft (go figure) and decided to placed a few air mattresses in the room and let out a few rooms to those who attended events in the region.

This is why you're getting the title AIR-BEDandBREAKFAST. It is not mandatory to offer breakfast when you're on this site So don't worry about the breakfast part of it scaring you. There's a humorous reason for their name since the first time they launched, they needed to raise funds for their website and they used sales to raise money. Specialty breakfast cereals such as "Obama-O's as well as Cap'N'Mcains". Fun and funny, it worked, as they managed to raise the capital needed to finance the launch of their website.

In the near future, AIRBNB offers a number of the same amenities like HomeAway including online bookings and security deposits however, there's a significant differences in other areas.

AIRBNB is more focused on the interaction between guests and host.

When you sign-up for the first time for the first time on AIRBNB you'll have to create a profile for yourself. This profile is where you'll be able to list things such as what your profession is, or what your personal hobbies are. This can be used to travel along with the profile (pun not intended). When you stay at the home of someone else on AIRBNB you will be able to evaluate you, and you'll be able to review them. When you host guests, they will look over your home and the way you manage it. This will be added to the profile you have created.

It's a far more personal experience as when you're booking guests , you will have a better understanding about them by looking through their profile, and look at their interests, as well as their reviews from the past.

The style of reviews that users post increases the trust factor that is compatible with the way the sharing economy functions. It's an organic feel which I believe is a place HomeAway isn't quite as good in.

They also include the automated Price Tip system in place which compares your home's price with similar properties in the area and also analyzes the demand and provides you with suggestions on the price you should sell your house at. I find the idea unique, and should you be new to selling your house, it's an excellent option to consider.

But I've discovered that it's usually a bit lower than the one about my house. As the system accumulates more data it will provide more precise numbers. It's an excellent beginning point to get your home noticed.

In certain cities, AIRBNB will hire a photographer to take photos of your home. This is a great benefit to have since high-quality images, which we'll cover in future chapters, are an essential aspect of having an effective listing.

Another major difference that you should be expecting in AIRBNB can be found in the fact that they see a younger generation smaller groups, as well as shorter durations. The typical booking time is closer to their travel dates, meaning just one or two months in advance. You can also opt to lease out rooms through AIRBNB and that's why it's an beneficial option for solo travelers.

I've also observed that since most those who list on AIRBNB reside in their homes and rent rooms, guests may anticipate a more interaction by the hosts. There is however the option of setting your listing to indicate that you're not listed present on the premises, something is something you should consider doing as we're trying to make the business as far away from operational as they can be.

This is the area where AIRBNB stands out from other options because they concentrate heavily on guest and host interaction so if you're hoping for a more personal experience with your guests, AIRBNB is the best spot to shine. They will encourage guests to be at the house at the time guests arrive and guide them around your home and perhaps even serve in the role of a tour guide for the city. If this sounds like something you would love to do, I would highly recommend placing your listing your property on AIRBNB.

Smaller rooms, affordability urban areas condos, and the personal interaction with guests shines on AIRBNB.

Other things to look out for are that AIRBNB in the moment of writing, will only allow you to make use of the Contract option.

One thing I typically do is to send my contract via email and ask the guest to sign it.

AIRBNB is completely free to advertise on, but they charge an amount of the reservation at 3% from the host, and they also charge guests between 6% and 12 percent, based on the total cost that the guest is paying for.

The way the system operates is that the higher the amount of the reservation the less the percent that AIRBNB will receive on behalf of guests.

I've had plenty of success using AIRBNB as host and avid traveler. I really like the sense of personal belonging they've sought to build.

While traveling through it has brought me in contact with some wonderful hosts, from those who have allowed me to use their surfboards and even swam with me, to one host who allowed me to stay on his sailboat while we talked about sailing around the world , and the pleasures and challenges that go from sailing.

It's difficult to recreate the same experience in motels or hotels which is the thing that AIRBNB is all about. They're creating an experience that's both for the host and the guest, more as any other business I've seen.

This is both ways. As an example I've hosted two sets of grandparents taking a trip across the country and into town to meet their family's brand-new granddaughter. I had a great time talking to them and even got an amazing photograph of the baby girl.

If you're interested in hosting through AIRBNB which I highly recommend take a look at this link. It's not just a direct link to the host setup , but you'll get fifty dollars the first time you try hosting with me!

A lesser-known listing website for vacation rentals that offers an option to list for free with an 3% booking cost. I've had listings with them prior to when they changed to a pay-per-book option.

I did not have any success with them, however, I had already been pretty firmly anchored to homeaway and vrbo when I started.

If you're just beginning to set off, don't hesitate to advertise your house to as many different options as you can. Once you've figured out what sites are the most suitable for your particular location, you'll be able to look through the useless websites for listing.

Here are a few choices I suggest you think about when planning your vacation rental, with the top ones are VRBO, HOMEAWAY and AIRBNB.

Don't be tempted to take on all of the above options from the beginning. Get your house on the market and then use the rest as sources for the expansion of your business.

Craigslist

Yes, it's the original Craigslist platform. Many may feel that this platform is old-fashioned however, it has an active user base. It also allows you to advertise cities geographically. Therefore, if your home is located near an important city and could be a great place to go on a getaway, it might be beneficial to advertise within the area of your home to inform people about an upcoming weekend getaway. The three things you'll need when you're using Craigslist and it's done to speed up the process:

1. A Username from Craigslist

2. Google Chrome, which is a similar browser that of Internet Explorer or Mozilla Firefox.

3. Roof, which is available on rooof.com (this small, clever application is integrated to Chrome and will renew your Craigslist postings). Craigslist)

The process of posting or renew listings for Craigslist is an extremely exhausting process If you're planning to advertise your home nationwide on craigslist, you'll have to look through your listings and update hundreds listings manually. This will take a lot longer than you would like to spend. That's the point where Roof comes into play.

Roof is utilized for real estate brokers in order to advertise homes they have to sell or property managers who manage rental properties but you could also use it to rent out vacation homes.

It's as easy as integrating it to Chrome and then switch it on, and it will renew your posts. You'll need to write the post before it goes live however, it will allow you to keep your posts up for the length of time you want without having to keep the posts up to date.

* SOCIAL MEDIA

It is here that things can become very exciting and entertaining in conversations. There aren't many homes I have come across use social media for marketing. I'm not talking about just visiting Facebook and possibly you can put their post on the wall of someone else's as an inexpensive form of advertisement. I'm talking about complete engagement with customers and the full immersion of them through integrating Twitter, Instagram, and Facebook in one, and creating a brand awareness for your property as well as a social following.

Imagine a crowd of people enjoying a good time sitting on your back patio, relaxing on your outdoor couches, enjoying meals from the grill Everyone is having a blast and having fun. Someone pulls out their smartphone and begins a video of the event. They then post their video to Instagram or Facebook with the hashtag the home you live in is listed as.

BAM! Instant marketing for your home , from those who are guests. Anyone who's looking through you Instagram hashtag will be able to see the video of your guests enjoying themselves at your house. Your advertising can't be more authentic than this.

If you're not familiar with much regarding social media I'll provide a brief overview and also suggest some websites that can provide you with more information and tricks about how to infusing it into your life.

The first and most important thing to remember is that hashtags -------> # <------- are all-encompassing. Consider them as categories or groups inside the binder. It's the binder, and hashtags represent the groups inside the binder. If someone uploads photos or videos that uses your hashtag it will be instantly added to the group. This means that everyone can contribute to the group, and anyone on Instagram will be able to see the posts the guests of yours have shared.

If a guest heads out and snaps a photo of a stunning waterfall or park close to your house and then posts it on your home's hashtag, immediately people who might be thinking of staying at your house will be able to see an awesome waterfall or park within walking distance of your house.

In essence, you're leaving your guests to do the marketing for the benefit of. The only thing you need to accomplish is making them be aware of your online media presence. It's possible to do this by a variety of methods like in your welcome emails , make sure to include your Instagram hashtag, your Twitter profile or Facebook page to let guests know that if they're at your home and would like to share photos on your profile, they're able to simply use your hashtag. Let's look at other strategies that can be used to boost your home's visibility through Facebook as well as Instagram.

Virtual Brochure

Share information about events and suggestions for the area. This can be done via Instagram and then link your posts onto your Facebook profile, too.

If you can show people the worth of the place they could be in, you're giving them tangible reasons to stay with you. Eventually, this will lead them one step closer to viewing your homes which they could rent in the region.

Travel bloggers

Consider integrating your company's Instagram or Facebook profiles with local travel writers. If they're already discussing the region It's an easy move for them to chat about the best vacation homes within the region. It can be an opportunity for everyone by advertising his blog.

Focus Your Demographic

In subsequent chapters, you'll be able explore ways to consider who you're targeting , and how to do it on social media.

This is the ideal time to focus on them in particular. If you're marketing your residence to the younger generation Consider including photos of exciting events that have an audience of younger people attached to it or how your home offers new facilities that are geared towards younger generations or the way your home is placed for young people.

Amenities

It's an ideal time to add some stunning photos of the features of your home. Imagine how awesome it would be an Instagram posting of an espresso in your breakfast area just when the sun is about to come to an end. Would you consider that to be a fantastic method of attracting people to the kind of experience your home could provide? Do you.

Testimonials

The inclusion of testimonials in your social media posts is a smart way to spread the word about how wonderful the home you live in is. If you've had someone leave you a glowing review that went into the specifics of what makes your house unique, then you should promote your baby on social media.

Discounted Rates

One of the most obvious ways is to include the discounted rates you offer in your social media posts. How better to gain more followers and more active engagement than to let them know that your house is set to go up for sale at a reduced price.

Hashtag your postings

A single of the crucial steps to take when you want to make your posts more visible on INSTAGRAM is to use Hashtags in all of your posts. What it does is spread your picture to these categories, so that people who are looking through them will be able to find your post and hence your profile.

Contests to Increase User Engagement

User engagement is an important factor in social marketing. One of the methods to encourage the engagement of users is to host contests where your guests share photos throughout their stay.

If you include the photo of them, they'll get an overnight stay for free towards an upcoming booking or something you think could provide a great reward.

Promoting your photos via hashtags

If you upload a photo of a beach that is great near your home, you might be able to include #vacationrental#beach"nameoftown" #ocean #homeaway "airbnb. These are very popular hashtags that help to make sure that your post is found.

What I'd suggest to do to determine the hashtags you can use for each post is to first and foremost to consider the relevance. There's no reason to mention #skiing if you're sharing a photo of relaxing in the desert

Do a second search on Instagram and look at which hashtags have the highest number of posts. Which ones that have the highest number of posts is the one that have the highest activity. We'd like to advertise our brand in hashtags that are active and have lots of activity in order to improve the chances of being discovered.

Here are some examples of the hashtags I've observed to be the most popular and that are designed for rental properties.

#airbnb

#homeaway

#homeawayfromhome

#vacationrental

#vacationrentals

#vacation

Vacation rentals are visually appealing and therefore Instagram is an ideal place to advertise your business. In the hashtags mentioned, AIRBNB has by far the most active posts from users on Instagram. Homeaway and vrbo don't seem very active on their social media platforms and this could be strange. However, when you consider that AIRBNB targets a younger crowd, it makes an amount of sense.

INSTAGRAM TIP

At present, there's no method to control hashtags. If you're concerned about who will publish what content to your hashtag I suggest to let people tag you with an Instagram account instead.

Then , you can select the photos you would like to display. This can be done by going to the settings section of the right side of your Instagram username and ensuring that your photos are approved by manual approval.

This isn't as accessible to guests who might be interested However, it's still an excellent method to capture the authentic moments you want to share with your guests, with a some security.

For example, instead of saying #hashtagyourvacationrental, tell them to tag whatever your Instagram username is and then when people do that you can choose which ones you want to have shown.

Twitter

Twitter is a great method to advertise openings on your calendar as well as promotions and events happening in your local area. Get your guests' email addresses and then post your twitter account's name to ensure that if guests would like to follow what you post, they'll get updates whenever you post.

For example when you are open for four days in the summer, you can inform all your followers on Twitter. You could also connect your Instagram hashtags to your twitter account to allow people to view videos and images of the happenings in your home.

Facebook

A majority of people have accounts on Facebook nowadays, but is it your home? This is also all about promoting social brand awareness to promote your house. Make a Facebook page for your home , where you can share pictures, videos, offers and stay in touch with guests you have recently hosted as well as past guests. Most importantly, you can connect the URLs of your Instagram as well as Twitter posts and name from this.

Take all of these effective social media tools and keep in mind the top listing sites you have including AIRBNB as well as Homeaway. Integrate them into your listings on these sites. By making sure that the hashtags of your Instagram account's hashtag, username or twitter account and facebook accounts included in the listings you have, you'll be able to promote your property with genuine interactions from your guests and be able to send the information out to those who are interested in the offers you'll be offering at your house.

I can assure you now that few homeowners who incorporate social media in their listings as this. Making these changes will to distinguish your home from the other homes.

Social Cause

This business is part of the sector called"sharing" economy. Are you interested in knowing something widespread about this field? Many businesses have a social purpose attached to their activities. The millennial generation is awestruck by this charitable endeavor. Imagine TOMS footwear and the one-for-one. For every pair of shoes they sell, they give one to a child in need. There are many other companies that offer a portion of their earnings to help provide drinking water for those who are in dire need, or food to hungry children.

Like I said earlier, this venture is very important on its own when you've established your"why" in earlier chapters. Add the social aspect and you're taking it an entirely new level. This is the reason I give an amount of income I earn from my home for Habitat For Humanity. I prefer to refer to it as the:

"Stay in a home-help create a Home" act.

If your home is having a great success, why not use that success into an occasion to assist others. At the end of the day you'll have a fantastic satisfaction from your business , knowing that you're helping others, and you'll also gain publicity.

This will cause people to feel compelled to buy your house because they'll feel as if they're doing something positive around the world. In a business sense, it's also tax-deductible.

* Website

This is a great way you can begin to show your personal brand. It could lead to lots of venture opportunities that you can create by using your homes. I'm developing my own website as I write this book. I've come across a number of useful sources to help you create your website ..., which isn't even talking about making the Geocities site (kudos to those who are aware of what I'm speaking about).

Lodgify

This is a great option for owners of vacation rentals with a minimal HTML background information or wish to know how to create their own website. There are a variety of templates that you can choose from and they're all made specifically for rental properties.

The website will also have some really nice features, like the ability to book your appointments and the ability to sync your calendars with the website reviews system, and numerous other features.

The most effective formula is that for majority of the time you'll in a position to drag and click the layout of your site and you'll be able to tell it's optimized in a way that are suitable for rental properties.

The monthly cost is about nineteen dollars per month for a single site that has a booking system as well as mobile optimized. Given how many users are browsing their mobiles, no matter which website you choose to use you'll need to ensure it's mobile-friendly. With the ease of making this is definitely an affordable price.

They offer their services at a reduced price by clicking this link.

http://bit.ly/lodgifyvacation

Wix

This could be one of the fastest and most straightforward options to build websites, and one that still looks great. There are a lot of pre-designed templates for websites that you can buy and connect to a massive collection of stock images they already have set up.

The price isn't too high and for those who don't have an extensive HTML backgrounds, you don't have to be concerned since generally, you're using the dashboard of your website , not designing it. WIX websites are created using focused on drag and drop.

Consider, for instance, your operating system Windows and Mac OS. It doesn't require computer programmers to utilize the computer since these operating systems can flesh out the coding , making it attractive and simple to navigate. Wix is like that with regards to the creation of websites.

Because WIX functions a lot like an operating system , you will not have the same flexibility in creating your site to the exact style you'd like

WordPress

If WordPress was an operating system It would be similar to Linux that has more flexibility in the way you can tailor it to meet your requirements and, as a result it comes with some learning curve.

You can build whatever you'd like from WordPress and then tailor it to your needs.

Although it does have some learning curves however, when you go to the WordPress website, you'll meet a lot of people who are willing to help you get your website moving in the proper direction.

For starters, WordPress has this thing called Themes. This is very like templates that WIX uses, however Themes are more flexible.

When you're looking over the theme you're considering, you can check out a demo to see what it might look like. If you're looking for an WordPress theme specifically designed for hotels but can be used to create an easy-to-use Blog section, you'll select a theme that you believe will work with that style.

After that, you are able to customize the Widgets that are included in the Theme. They are basically similar to apps that you can download for your phone. They let you add items on your site like large images that slide, or a booking system, an RSS feed for Social Media or blogs feeds, weather alerts , etc.

It might seem a bit crazy to you at the moment But there are several websites that you can visit to get more information about creating your WordPress website.

Lynda.com

Skillshare.com

Coursera.com

youtube.com

If you choose to buy a theme which I would recommend doing typically, they'll have their website and forums with instructions step-by-step for setting up their themes.

99designs

The company can be found below in Logo Design, which is their main focus, however they can also create your website. As a bonus they'll link the design of your website to the logo of your company. If you don't want to create it on your own. This could be the solution you're seeking.

* Logo Design

If you would like to expand to more holiday rentals or think that a website might be coming up then having a Logo is a great idea to give people an image to connect to your properties. While I'm no professional graphic artist, however I've come across several websites that are great for branding your business in the future.

Fiverr

I've had lots of success with Fiverr. It's a simple and simple way to search for and obtain the logo you want. It may not be unique in every aspect however it's an effective logo. What you'll need to do is browse through the list of graphic designers who detail their work so you'll know the kinds of designs you like , and then place an order with your company's name or slogan. The most exciting part is that, most of the time, you can get all this done for less than $30 dollars.

99designs

This is the best choice to get the work done in a unique way.

The way they work (no pun intended) is that you'll start the contest with a graphic during the time frame of approximately one week. There will be a variety of designs that are sent to you. You can pick which you like, and then work with the designer directly to improve it further.

This is quite some more but you'll most likely spend several hundred dollars on the design of your logo with this process, but usually you'll get an image that is more like what you can see in your head.

If you choose to browse to 99designs I strongly recommend you read their guide on what constitutes an excellent branding design. The survey is short and contains around eight questions to be asked to answer, and at the end, you'll have an improved brand idea that the designers can work with. If you get your designs, they'll be close to what you're hoping for your brand to portray.

* Free Photography

Did you know have the option that AIRBNB will send an expert photographer to photograph your house for free? The offer is only available to specific regions, meaning your listing might not be considered eligible. To check if it is, go over to www.airbnb.com/info/photography and see if your listing at the bottom is available.

The disadvantage of using the services of an AIRBNB photographer is that the pictures are taken over by AIRBNB and AIRBNB, meaning they'll be able to use them as they want however you won't actually get the photos. Instead, they'll be uploaded to your listing once they're all complete. The beggars aren't the only ones to choose.

* Pets

The two HomeAway and Airbnb have choices to determine if they allow animals or do not. For one of my homes I allow pets. In my more luxurious home, I don't allow pets as I do not want to risk harm to my home as well as the fact that, I make it clear that it is an ideal place to live in for those who suffer from allergies. However, I allow dogs to my less expensive home because it is a way to accommodate those who simply cannot keep their pets their home while to vacation.

If you're planning to permit pets, I recommend the use of a small pet damage fund to be prepared for the worst or perhaps charging an additional fee for pets to cover the risk.

* Minimum Stays

In the majority of properties I've managed or owned the minimum stay was usually three days. I'm aware that in some regions that they have minimum stay requirements during peak season, which can be up to a whole week. I've found 3 days to be a decent average for my area. But based on the location you're in it could be that it's better to opt for an extended minimum.

Be aware that certain regions have rules in place which require you to keep an amount of time per reservation. Therefore, regardless of what, you may be required to rent your home one week at a given time in accordance with rules.

In the off-season for me, it's been apparent an increase in my daily minimum hours down to two days helps attract more weekend visitors and fill days that would otherwise be empty.

The home you live in and the price, I wouldn't recommend an all-day minimum. The main reason I'm wary of this is because it can give the party-goers a greater chance of being targeted. One way to stop this kind of thing from happening is to have an extended minimum stay as well as the option of a good damage deposit.

Chapter 7: Interior Design

I'd like to mention two essential points to keep in mind when planning your vacation rental. In the first place, you must consider the practicality of the space How will guests use this space or moving into or out of this area of the house and who will use this space. We'll discuss this in greater depth in the near future.

Another aspect, which I feel it's just as crucial as the idea of design. What I am referring to is once we've got our function of the space it is then time be thinking about the best way to create a mood using the use of amenities including furniture, colors, and furniture and how place the room in order to help create an ambience.

Companies are discovering increasingly that being able to use the service is not enough. Studies have shown that businesses that have focused on the design aspects of their products or services have experienced as high as an increase of 10% in sales due to it.

There are many holiday rentals that are focused on the function of their homes. They'll furnish their living space with a couple of nifty pieces of furniture that meet the basic needs of every room, however the guests leave feeling that the space is unfinished and the owner only cares about their needs.

We often overlook the indirect significance of our actions and only looking at the function and basic requirements of our rooms, we're communicating something to potential guests.

The wide array of emotions guests experience by the choices you make in designing your home could bring about more reservations and rave reviews or negative intent and a few reservations. Small things like the color of your ceilings could make rooms appear smaller or spacious.

Another reason is that you may have your personal possessions and photographs scattered throughout the house. This could make it difficult for guests to feel comfortable and make them feel like they're at the home of someone else. We're not looking for the impression of a hotel that is sterile We still desire to bring our own personal traits to our home however not in a way that is a hindrance to feeling of being at home.

When we're considering interior design, we should keep in mind that we're trying to create the style and function to create a mood for every one of our rooms. It's important to bring you the feeling you're looking for.

When people spend more time in your home, they'll begin to notice the smallest details you incorporate in your house that bring positive feelings and you can recall these through a few fundamental ideas that define interior style: functionality of a room as well as the mood of a room. Let's look at these concepts and subcategories so that you'll have a more thorough understanding of the things you'll want to consider when designing your holiday home.

* Functionality

There are some things I prefer to concentrate on when it comes to the practicality of the room the people who will use this space, why do they want to use this space, and how everything fit into the space.

Who's Using It?

Going back to the section about how to reach our Target Demographic, we should already have a accurate idea of the kinds of people we'll be inviting to our home. I'll take one of my houses as an illustration. I was certain that because of my location and the design of my house that it would be a perfect family home. That's why I wanted to have a functional home is a good idea. It's also a good fit in line with the family's requires and wants to do on vacation.

Let's take a few rooms and consider ways to create a productive space for a family. The house is quite large and is able to accommodate a huge family gathering, and more likely, multi-generational. This is why, within the Living Room, I wanted to make sure that I could have enough seating for this bigger crowd.

And, of course, I knew that families are likely to have children. This is why I wanted to create an area where the kids could go to as well as parents can escape to. Therefore, I transformed the basement into an space of entertainment by incorporating a toy box with a game console, the air hockey game, Hoole hoops and various other things to keep the kids entertained and parents at peace upstairs.

To top it off but, within this setting, I created a perfect space to gather with friends and play pool, or enjoy a show. This is a perfect place for the guys in the family to unwind and unwind.

There are some possibilities Now, I was considering a house and came across an amazing home that I was contemplating purchasing.

One thing I considered to be a cool aspect was the fact that the house had a shack located in the backyard. The house was a fantastic fence around it, plenty of grass and space for kids to run around on.

What I imagined would make an awesome, unique feature for this home is to convert the shack to an awesome playland/movie theater for children. I thought of a great TV, an awesome toy box and castles that kids could play in.

Imagine a truly castle-themed experience for them that they could easily access in the backyard. The kind of experience you can imagine would be an appealing draw for prospective mothers browsing through listings. Keep in mind that, as per surveys that it is mothers of family who decides where to be the most times.

When it comes to functionality, we must think about who will be visiting our property, and the reasons for it. This way we can ensure that we provide an experience that is valuable to the customer we are targeting and, in the end, adding something unique which will help our establishment distinct from the thousands of other vacation rental homes.

The Focal Point

This was something I discussed within the photo chapter about the fact that every room is an focal area. It could be a fireplace or could be a glass window that has an amazing view. Whatever the case it is important to create a space that people's natural orientation will be guided toward. Yu accomplish this with aligning the furniture so that it makes it the normal way that people move.

The Furniture

When we're discussing the subject of furniture, we should keep in mind that not all pieces of furniture will work in every space. What I mean is that sometimes furniture regardless of how beautiful it appears can make an area appear small or can make a room appear excessively slender and empty. As an example when I was furnishing one of my houses, I was able to have a large L-seat couch that was brought into. The furniture also came with an additional piece at the back. The first time I bought it, I wanted everything.

However, what I noticed was that when I added the addition unit, it made the living space appear tiny and that's the last factor I had in mind because I know that families prefer homes with a spacious and open design.

So I decided to stay clear of the unit. Although it could add some seating, it created a feeling of being too small. My top priority is when my emotions are specifically targeted by something, I'd rather focus on it. If I feel good about it I'll be able to keep it. But, it's a no-no, and it should be thrown away no matter how lovely it would be to have.

In addition to making the space feel smaller and sluggish, it is common to find furniture that doesn't make sense for how big an area is. Are you expecting your guests to glance at your photos and notice that you only have one bamboo chair within a 400 square foot space? Absolutely it's not. The truth is the overwhelming emotion people are going to feel while in the room, or watching the photos. They may be thinking this is a very basic, bare/chintzy/sparse place and all the negative adjectives you can imagine.

Make sure your home is well-furnished and you'll get the return you put into your home.

Additionally, there are lots of questions regarding the kinds of furniture that one can purchase. It's quite common to see holiday homes that are furnished with affordable but durable furniture which makes sense in terms of the overhead cost.

But, I would recommend you to go against the current trend in this. There are many vacation rentals available that are brimming with cheap furniture. There's nothing wrong with choosing to incorporate some style or luxury in your rental properties.

Many people are concerned about furniture getting damaged So here's what I would suggest.

For couches, loungers and other seating options choose a microfiber material. It first and foremost is stunning. Furthermore, it's one of the easiest materials to clean and eliminate the stains. So, you can enjoy an attractive appearance and sturdy material that you can quickly remove stains from.

For your dining table Consider quartz or granite. It's not as stain-resistant as marble, or is an extremely sturdy wood such as maple, mahogany, walnut or oak. Another option that is a good fit for a design that is modern and clean is glass tables. These are all fantastic ideas which will last for a long time and look stunning.

It's something I'm constantly struggling with in my vacation rental properties. For instance, I've always would like to revamp the kitchen completely, and one thing I've considered is installing the butcher block counters.

They look stunning and make a perfect addition to this home. But , after some investigation I've discovered that they're susceptible to cuttings, water stains and a myriad of other issues. For now, I've decided not to use the same type of countertop in the near future kitchen remodel unless I find an option to increase their durability.

Sleeping Accommodations

Everyone wants comfortable bed, and you shouldn't get low-cost [Glow3] on them. It's pretty simple to understand, but I'd like to concentrate on another thing that is how many people you can accommodate in your house. Being able to sleep more in a variety of ways is beneficial, up to a certain degree. It's fairly obvious that if your house can accommodate ten people,

Then, those ten will likely to share the cost, and you could be charged more however it'll still be fairly affordable for them.

There's a limit to what you can do in this kind of thinking and it's easy to make this decision solely on the property. But that's not the only thing that you have to think about. It is also important to be thinking about parking. How many cars could you put in your driveway as well as on the sidewalk? Are you blocking the neighbor's parking spot? It's a simple and simple way to receive complaints, and possibly have your vacation rental closed.

Additionally, is the style of the home sufficient to be able to hold that many people? Most older homes don't have the open layout that allows them to handle large groups.

Are you able to use enough bathroom facilities? A large number of people are likely to get up early and usually need to shower and get prepared for the morning. Ten people in one bathroom is an unimaginable task. To top it off do you have a water heater big enough to handle the load?

There is also the possibility of turning into the party venue and becoming damaged when you have large groups.

In terms of money, it's an excellent benefit to have a sufficient to sleep arrangements for larger numbers, as long as it doesn't become an event. If you do choose to do this, take into consideration all the aspects of a large gathering on your property, including parking, their arrival, exit and movement through your home, potential noise in addition to the increased wear and tear on your home, and seating arrangements.

You're offering a place to live Yes.

However, your home isn't the only element that is an aspect of the experience. everything else in the surroundings is tied to this particular experience, for example, the way your neighbors will be affected by the increased traffic.

* Mood

Another important thing to be aware of alongside functionality is mood. This can be achieved through various ways, starting with the colors we choose to use. The kind of lighting we choose as well as the type of furniture or the arrangement of our home, the decor we choose to add, as well as the scent that we put in our house. In this regard we must look through it from the perspective of our psychological wellbeing.

Every aspect of a home triggers emotions of some kind. For instance, did be aware that recent studies have discovered that the ceiling's height influence how you think? According to research, 10 feet or higher, you'll think more abstractly. Ten feet or less and you'll concentrate more on specific relationships.

This isn't a way to tell you to build your walls bigger or lower. I'm simply making this an example for you to see the way that even small things can impact our mood. The thing that is interesting about the study is that this isn't directly related to what the space actually is, but rather how we imagine it to be. This, my dears, is the area that most of us are capable of playing in to change the way an area feels without having to physically recreate the space.

Theme

When it comes down to setting my mood I prefer to begin by considering the general Theme I'd like to build on. The most important thing to consider when designing interiors is the way in which things flow between rooms. It's certainly not a bad idea to create themed rooms that alter and change and change, it can be quite enjoyable. For the majority of us, there's an overall theme for our house, and it should be consistent from room to room. That being said which kind of home do we want to build here? Are we building an elegant American Craftsman? A beach bungalow? An artsy draw? A contemporary home? A home for sailors on the sea? Pick one while letting the remainder evolve out of it.

"The best interiors of today and in the past are those that are able to be compared to their character and are appropriate to the building in question."

For the majority of us, the theme will be determined by the place we live in our home , or by the design of the home it self. Whatever the initial design of your home the best way to incorporate it into it and emphasize that overall theme. For instance, if you own the look of a craftsman-style home, it's best to avoid turning it into an Spanish Adobe style home.

Accessory Items

If we consider the theme of our room What are some important elements that can increase the scale? If you're planning an ocean-themed home and you have a few surfboards, hanging them up could be a good feature. If you're going for a nautical theme it's great to include a sailboat or a large number of blue-striped pillows in. There are numerous ways to connect things to common themes and integrate the theme into your home. This is a great way to bring your own individuality to the home , so that it will always be an original draw.

Lighting

Lighting will be an issue across your house. How does light impact our mood?

There is an reason why we dim the lights to create an intimate setting. Many studies have revealed that dim lighting can make us feel more relaxed and relaxed. While bright lighting can help us stay conscious and alert however, it could also make us feel uncomfortable. Make note of what areas of your house you would like to set a certain mood in. In the event that you own a lovely study area, it would be sensible to ensure that the lighting is sufficient to allow reading, but not so bright that it makes people feel anxious and uncomfortable.

Furniture Placement

Where you place your furniture will play a major role. We know, for instance, that we'd like to have an accent piece, but we must also make sure that we don't create an area appear too small.

The room is either sparse or overly dense or over. When you're walking through the space, be aware of the way people move around the room , and what they'll be doing. If it's an area for socializing it is important to try and arrange the seating in a way that is appropriate for the event. A circle-shaped seating arrangement in this instance is more appropriate than seating adjacent to it.

* Colors

There's a long list of ways colors affect our mood. I'll go through making a list of the most well-known colors and the way they tend to affect the way people feel. I enjoy thinking about the branding of companies with regards to colors. There's a reason behind why certain brands or industries are more likely to employ certain colors.

* Blue

It is a unanimous choice to bring a sense tranquility and freshness to the space. It's typically associated with a secure and comfortable sensation. It is common to see Blues in bathrooms as well as in kitchens, bedrooms and bathrooms.

* Red

A bold hue that commands attention. You'll see it frequently linked to passion, strength and love. It's also used to stimulate the senses.

There are many people who wear red accent pieces on drapery or chairs.

Something that adds a touch of pizazz to the room. In actuality I blend red and its various shades into many different rooms in my home.

Sometimes, I'll see some red hues on my pillows for throws or paintings or even draperies to give a sense of elegance and regality to the surroundings.

* Yellow

It can bring a sense of positivity and joy in an atmosphere. It can help in promoting understanding of communication, and it's an excellent idea to think about the use of it in places that host social gatherings.

* Orange

Another color that can give the room an impression of excitement and energy. Most often, Orange is used similarly to red but as an accent color than a primary color, since it can be overwhelming when utilized too often.

* Green

It can give any space an air of cleanliness and fresh. It's also linked to the renewal of life, which leads to a positive and calming sensation.

* Black

This color can give the appearance of elegance or glamour. Most of the time, it's utilized for the decoration of kitchen appliances. The black and white chair juxtaposed with the red cushion is an effective way to convey to anyone who is watching with enthusiasm. There are plenty of creative ways to mix colours to bring out the emotion that you're seeking.

These are just a few of the ideas and the psychology behind the most popular colors.

Keep in mind that even though we have our basic colors but we also have our colors too. Blue can give you a feeling of calm. If you add the opposite and add a darker hue to the blue color, you begin to feel like you are feeling more of a dull feeling rather than the light and tranquil.

The bottom line is that we'll want keep track of what different types of colors we're using and in relation to the photographs that we have in our homes.

If you're going to take one idea from this chapter on interior design you should take into consideration that people are attracted by COLOR.

We must remember that these rooms have to appear good on camera.

One of the most effective ways to catch the attention of others is to choose the perfect combination of colors that make you stand out.

Most of us, we're drawn to the colors in nature, like reds, blues and yellows browns, beige and blues which aren't overly aggressive and are readily available in the natural world. Most of the time, these will be the best choice when it comes to picking colours.

For tips and suggestions on how to ensure that you use the correct mix of shades, recommend using the color wheel.

Color Wheel

A color wheel can aid in integrating several colors within one room.

It can be something that is difficult however, the use of a color wheel can aid in making the whole procedure easy. It is based on the colors blue, yellow, and red and their various shades. There are basically three kinds of hues.

Primary Colors

The three colors, blue, and red in traditional color theory are the primary colors and three pigments which cannot be mixed or created in any other colors. All other colors originate from these three hues.

Secondary Colors

Orange, green and purple are the colors created by mixing primary colors.

Tertiary Colors

Yellow-orange, red-orange, red-purple, blue-purple, blue-green & yellow-green. These are the hues created when you mix a primary color with an additional color. This is the reason why the hue has an acronym with two words for blue-green, red violet, and yellow-orange.

www.ingramcontent.com/pod-product-compliance
Lightning Source LLC
Chambersburg PA
CBHW071223210326
41597CB00016B/1921